Lecture Notes in Computer Science 12130

More information about this series at http://www.springer.com/series/8637

Abdelkader Hameurlain · A Min Tjoa (Eds.)

Transactions on Large-Scale Data- and Knowledge-Centered Systems XLIII

 Springer

Editors-in-Chief
Abdelkader Hameurlain
IRIT, Paul Sabatier University
Toulouse, France

A Min Tjoa
Vienna University of Technology
Vienna, Austria

ISSN 0302-9743   ISSN 1611-3349   (electronic)
Lecture Notes in Computer Science
ISSN 1869-1994   ISSN 2510-4942   (electronic)
Transactions on Large-Scale Data- and Knowledge-Centered Systems
ISBN 978-3-662-62198-1   ISBN 978-3-662-62199-8   (eBook)
https://doi.org/10.1007/978-3-662-62199-8

This Springer imprint is published by the registered company Springer-Verlag GmbH, DE
part of Springer Nature
The registered company address is: Heidelberger Platz 3, 14197 Berlin, Germany

Preface

This volume contains five fully revised selected regular papers, covering a wide range of very hot topics in the fields of machine learning algorithms for classification tasks, top-k queries over distributed uncertain categorical data, cost-based optimization solutions for business processes, a knowledge capitalization framework in the big data context, and building a multilingual disease-news profiler.

We would like to sincerely thank the Editorial Board and the external reviewers for thoroughly refereeing the submitted papers and ensuring the high quality of this volume.

Special thanks go to Gabriela Wagner for her availability and her valuable work in the realization of this TLDKS volume.

May 2020

Abdelkader Hameurlain
A Min Tjoa

Organization

Editors-in-Chief

Abdelkader Hameurlain   IRIT, Paul Sabatier University, France
A Min Tjoa   Technical University of Vienna, Austria

Editorial Board

Reza Akbarinia   Inria, France
Dagmar Auer   FAW, Austria
Djamal Benslimane   Claude Bernard University Lyon 1, France
Stéphane Bressan   National University of Singapore, Singapore
Mirel Cosulschi   University of Craiova, Romania
Dirk Draheim   Tallinn University of Technology, Estonia
Johann Eder   University of Klagenfurt (AAU), Austria
Anastasios Gounaris   Aristotle University of Thessaloniki, Greece
Theo Härder   Technical University of Kaiserslautern, Germany
Sergio Ilarri   University of Zaragoza, Spain
Petar Jovanovic   Universitat Politècnica de Catalunya, BarcelonaTech, Spain
Dieter Kranzlmüller   Ludwig-Maximilians-Universität München, Germany
Philippe Lamarre   INSA Lyon, France
Lenka Lhotská   Technical University of Prague, Czech Republic
Vladimir Marik   Technical University of Prague, Czech Republic
Jorge Martinez Gil   Software Competence Center Hagenberg, Austria
Franck Morvan   IRIT, Paul Sabatier University, France
Torben Bach Pedersen   Aalborg University, Denmark
Günther Pernul   University of Regensburg, Germany
Soror Sahri   LIPADE, Descartes Paris University, France
Shaoyi Yin   Paul Sabatier University, France
Feng (George) Yu   Youngstown State University, USA

External Reviewers

Guillaume Cabanac   IRIT, Paul Sabatier University, France
Julius Köpke   University of Klagenfurt (AAU), Austria
Riad Mokadem   IRIT, Paul Sabatier University, France

Contents

Role-Based Access Classification: Evaluating the Performance of Machine Learning Algorithms

Randy Julian[2], Edward Guyot[2], Shaowen Zhou[2], Geong Sen Poh[2], and Stéphane Bressan[1(✉)]

[1] National University of Singapore, Singapore, Singapore
steph@nus.edu.sg
[2] NUS-Singtel Cyber Security R&D Laboratory, Singapore, Singapore

Abstract. The analysis of relational database access for the purpose of audit and anomaly detection can be based on the classification of queries according to user roles. One such approach is DBSAFE, a database anomaly detection system, which uses a Naïve Bayes classifier to detect anomalous queries in Role-based Access Control (RBAC) environments. We propose to consider the usual machine learning algorithms for classification tasks: K-Nearest Neighbours, Random Forest, Support Vector Machine and Convolutional Neural Network, as alternatives to DBSAFE's Naïve Bayes classifier. We identify the need for an effective representation of the input to the classifiers. We propose the utilisation of a query embedding mechanism with the classifiers. We comparatively and empirically evaluate the performance of different algorithms and variants with two benchmarks: the comprehensive off-the-shelf OLTP-Bench benchmark and a variant of the CH-benCHmark that we extended with hand-crafted user roles for database access classification. The empirical comparative evaluation shows clear benefits in the utilisation of the machine learning tools.

Keywords: Database · RBAC · Machine learning · Classification · DBSAFE · Benchmark · Query2Vec

1 Introduction

Classification of database access patterns has been studied and used to provide audit reports, to detect anomalous accesses and to detect insider threats.

One system that implements such an approach is DBSAFE. DBSAFE was introduced by Sallam *et al.* in [44]. DBSAFE uses a supervised machine learning classifier to classify queries according to the role of the users. It assumes the existence of a mechanism that can label the queries such as Role-based Access Control (RBAC). Queries are classified using features such as tables and attributes accessed, as well as their selectivity. Queries classified as a different role than that of the role of their user are flagged as anomalous. DBSAFE and its variants

A. Hameurlain and A Min Tjoa (Eds.): TLDKS XLIII, LNCS 12130, pp. 1–39, 2020.
https://doi.org/10.1007/978-3-662-62199-8_1

have been well researched [7,23,41,44–46] for the past few years and represent a state-of-the-art class of anomaly detection systems for databases. The original implementation of DBSAFE uses a Naïve Bayes classifier. It is natural and timely to ask whether other machine learning algorithms can improve the approach. We propose to compare the performance of the Naïve Bayes classifier with the usual machine learning algorithms for classification tasks, namely, K-Nearest Neighbours, Support Vector Machine, Random Forest and Convolutional Neural Network. DBSAFE uses a quadruplet representation of the queries. The Naïve Bayesian classifier allows this representation, which is slightly more structured than the usual feature vector used as input to other machine learning algorithms. It carries in a compact manner information that would otherwise require exponentially many features. We investigate the opportunity to use embedding techniques to circumvent this problem and represent structural aspects of the queries into a flat feature vector.

We use the OLTP-Bench benchmark and a variant of the CH-benCHmark to create synthetic datasets with meaningful hand-crafted roles to comparatively evaluate the performance of the different machine learning algorithms and techniques investigated.

The remainder of this paper is organised as follows. Section 2 discusses the related works, including anomaly detection systems in databases and creations of benchmark datasets for anomaly detection in databases. Section 3 summarises the necessary background on machine learning algorithms and feature vector representation for queries as well as introduces the benchmarking tool used for the creation of the datasets. Section 4 outlines our approach to the integration of different machine learning algorithms and of a query embedding mechanism into DBSAFE. Section 5 begins with descriptions of synthetic data creation before presenting and discussing the result of an extensive comparative empirical performance evaluation of the different machine learning models without and with the query embedding mechanism with the two synthetic datasets. We summarise our findings and outline future work in Sect. 6.

2   Related Works

One of the main applications of databases query classification is the detection of anomalies. As such in the following sections, we discuss the existing anomaly detection systems with descriptions of the classification techniques deployed in these works.

2.1   Anomaly Detection Systems for Databases

The use of anomaly detection systems for the purposes of audit and insider threat detection in databases has been addressed extensively in the literature. We begin with a recent paper by Sallam and Bertino [43]. The authors present a survey of prominent anomaly detection systems for database management systems and propose categories of feature spaces that can be used to study existing schemes.

According to the paper, features used for classification in anomaly detection for database management systems largely comprises of four main categories of feature spaces: syntax-based, data-centric, context-based and temporal. In this section, we will further divide the related works according to role-based and non role-based anomaly detection systems.

Non Role-Based Anomaly Detection Systems. The first category of anomaly detection systems looks at the interactions with the database without differentiating the role that the user belongs to.

Wu and Hung [17] proposed to use association rule mining, a data mining technique, to detect anomalies in database audit logs. The system uses syntactic and contextual features extracted from the audit logs. It mines and clusters association rules from the logs grouped by each user during training. When performing anomaly detection, it counts each log entry's mismatch with rule clusters and marks the log as an anomaly if the mismatch count is above some predefined threshold.

Chung *et al.* [12] proposed DEMIDS, a cluster-based detection system that uses the syntactic features of the queries. It is one of the first anomaly detection system targeted at databases. It gets information from the target database logs and the distance between features is manually defined by a security officer. It then uses this distance in order to compute sets of "close" features that are then used to define the normal behaviour of the users.

Hussain *et al.* [21] proposed DetAnom, an application-based detection system that combines syntactic and contextual features. The idea is to use concolic testing in order to find the constraints that lead to the application issuing each query. The system then detects anomalies by comparing the constraints of the issuing application to the possible constraint leading to the query sent. While focusing more on application tempering and exploitation, the paper also discusses how to use the run-time overhead as a metric to compare different approaches to database anomaly detection.

Singh *et al.* [50] proposed a syntactic based mechanism to detect malicious transactions by dynamically measuring the sensitivity of attributes and data dependency rules though mining frequent sequences of user's access pattern from audit logs. The features are extracted from the read/write sequences from audit logs and the sensitivity of the sequence's occurrences are then measured. The similarities between incoming sequences are then calculated to classify the malicious transaction.

Roichman and Gudes [38] proposed Diweda, a system to detect intrusions in web databases that also uses the syntactic information of the queries as well as temporal information based on users sessions. One major difference from other systems is that it targets users' connection sessions in order to detect anomalous SQL sessions from web applications. After query logs are divided by sessions, it builds session profiles for each access role. Access roles are learned by the system based on the assumption that every access role behaves different from each other. To identify different roles, the system first generates the fingerprint set from all queries and then encodes each session using a vector which indicates the appearance of fingerprints in the session. Afterwards, it clusters session vectors and regards each cluster as one role. During the detection phase, it flag the sessions which are far away from any cluster center as anomalies.

IBM InfoSphere Guardium's anomaly detection system combines the use of user profiles with past behaviour-based grouping of users. Mazzawi et al. [34] proposed a system integrated into IBM InfoSphere Guardium, based on collecting transactions of queries in a one-hour time frame. It divides each of those queries from an audit log by the type of query and table accessed, and then create vectors named atomic actions, consisting of groups of features from the query log for each of those sub-queries, like user's IP address, target database's name, target database's IP, timestamp, etc. The system consists of three phases: preprocessing, main algorithm and visualisation and feedback. The main algorithm consists of self-consistency and global-consistency models.

The self-consistency model computes the probability of the occurrence of the set of atomic actions for a user in the analysed time slice, based on the occurrence distribution of the known atomic actions, and estimated distribution of the occurrence of new atomic actions based on the model computed during training. The score is then normalised as the percentage of time slices encountered during training with a lower probability of occurring based on the model.

The global consistency model consists of a model that compute the distance between the behaviour of a user during a time slice and the behaviour expected from similar users. For that, we look at the user's activity during time slices as points in an n-th dimensional unit sphere, where each dimension represents an atomic action. We summarise the behaviour of each user during training by a vector in this space, representing the probability of the user doing each atomic action during a time slice. We can then cluster the users using K-means with cosine similarity distance. The anomaly score of each future time slices is then computed as a weighted L_2 norm that emphasises the atomic action with greater consensus inside the cluster.

Role-Based Anomaly Detection System. The second category of anomaly detection systems use the roles given by a Role-based Access Control mechanism as labels to use supervised machine learning for the detection.

Sallam and Bertino [42] proposed a data-centric and temporal based detection that can detect data aggregation and user's attempts to track data updates. For each role, it creates a profile of the access rate of retrieval for each tuple in the database based on the access rate of each user of that role. This system also uses a time-series with a sliding-window algorithm.

DBSAFE and the family of anomaly detection systems derived from it are the most relevant systems to the work presented by this paper.

Sallam et al. [7] proposed a system that uses the roles given by a Role-Based Access Control mechanism to label queries from the audit logs. The system looks at the audit logs one query at a time and extracts features from those queries. It then gets information on the query command type, table queried and column queried to create a triplet, the format used to record and process the information. It also gets the role of the user doing the query from the query and RBAC in order to use supervised learning on the resulting triplet. The feature extraction of this system has gone through multiple iterations. First, Sallam *et al.* proposed an improvement on the system by adding the information on the qualification component of the query, and the information includes the tables and columns used in the query predicate [23]. Ronao and Cho [39] proposed a random forest with weighted voting and principal component analysis as feature extraction and selection techniques. It relies on a clause-based view of the query to extract information on the clause and attribute features like the number of features present in each clause as well as position projection of those features in the query. It also relies on syntactic information like the length, number of string, number of JOIN and number of ANDs, ORs. The model also assumes RBAC in place. For the experiment, the paper utilised TPC-E schema and created two test datasets using uniform and Zipf distributions. Bu and Cho [10] proposed a convolutional neural network learning classifier system that is based on Role-Based Access Control mechanism. They utilised the feature extraction from Ronao and Cho [39] and further improved the feature selection process by introducing genetic algorithm and convolutional neural network as part of the discovery and performance components. The test dataset that they used was based on TPC-E schema and they conducted a 10-fold cross-validation tests and paired sample t-test to compare the accuracy and p-value.

Mathew *et al.* [33] demonstrated the limitations of the syntax-based approach on information extraction from queries. They proposed a user-based detection system that creates profiles of the users based on the statistical summary of the users' queries' results instead of on the queries themselves.

Shebaro *et al.* [49] then proposed to stop looking at the audit log files, and instead integrate their system directly inside PostgreSQL's database management system to leverage PostgreSQL's parser and get closer to the target. They reverted to using the triplet defined in [7].

Sallam *et al.* [44] proposed DBSAFE as a system that profiles users of the databases based on their roles. It assumes a Role-Based Access Control mechanism is in-place. The query is represented as a quadruplet. They used the idea from [49] of using the PostgreSQL database system's optimiser to get the parse tree of the query, but used a SQL proxy instead of fusing with the database management system. They added the selectivity approximation given by PostgreSQL's optimiser to the triplet from [7]. This information is then used to monitor data exfiltration. This system can be used for live monitoring of queries, and detect anomalous behaviour without needing to first execute the queries. Sallam and Bertino [46] published an improved version of DBSAFE [44] by suggesting various improvements to deal with limitations of DBSAFE. These include updating of the Naïve Bayes classifier and handling unbalanced data. They also introduced the use of Multi-labelling classifier to handle overlaps between roles. In the case where there is no clear role information, they suggested using unsupervised techniques to form clusters of users. While DBSAFE relies on PostgreSQL parser and optimiser, they introduced T-database management system adapters for Oracle and SQL Server. In the experiment, they created various test cases using Uniform and Zipf distributions. Sallam *et al.* [45] further improve on [46] by adding a way to handle the case where the database management system does not use Role-Based Access Control or that this feature is not available. In order to achieve that, they rely on unsupervised learning with COBWEB clustering to replace the role by the cluster of the user. Sallam and Bertino [41] proposed a system with three levels of anomaly detection. The first level is an online anomaly detection system that uses a lightweight DBSAFE with PostgreSQL's optimiser for query selectivity. This anomaly detection system provides real-time anomaly detection by assigning a score indicating the risk degree of each query before the query is executed by the database. Then periodically, it uses an offline lightweight DBSAFE implementation on the queries not flagged by the first level of detection. This second level of detection relies on the first one in order to compute a more precise selectivity. Finally, the last DBSAFE implementation aggregates the queries which are not flagged by the online anomaly detection system based on the database users' sessions in order to catch data aggregation that would not have been flagged otherwise.

2.2   Query Features and Representation

The effectiveness of the classification of queries for the purpose of anomaly detection depends on the features extracted from queries and used for the classification. Representation learning [5] tries to find a unified compressed feature vector representation of semi-structured input which captures certain relationships in original data automatically. This area is under extensive research in recent years, especially in natural language processing.

Hinton [19] introduced the idea of distributed representations. Following this, Bengio et al. [6] proposed word embedding to address the issue brought by the curse of dimensionality when learning the joint probability function of sequences of words in a language. Mikolv et al. [35,36] published an efficient algorithm called word2vec, and demonstrated good quality of the representations generated by the algorithm in a word similarity task. Le and Mikolov [26] extended word2vec to doc2vec which finds representations for documents and sentences. LSTM [20], which is a recurrent neural network architecture, has also been used in various representation learning tasks including text autoencoders [29] and machine translation [32]. Jain et al. [22] proposed two methods, doc2vec and LSTM autoencoder, as underlying methods of Query2Vec and evaluated the performance of query representations for workload summarisation and classification tasks.

2.3   Dataset and Synthetic Data Creation

We consider application benchmarks with their synthetic datasets as the experiments can easily be replicated and scaled. A workload generator creates the schema and populate the database.

Sallam and Bertino [7, 23] create statistical models of the synthetic workloads by defining the probability of using a command c given a role r, the probability of projecting to table t given the role r and command c, etc. The probabilities are generated using different distributions such as uniform, Zipf, reverse Zipf and multinomial.

In their more recent papers, Sallam and Bertino used the workload from OLTP-Bench benchmark [16] to generate datasets for their experiments. Sallam *et al.* [46] used workloads from benchmarks such as TPC-C, Epinions and TATP. However, in this paper, they did not look at the role of the users and only used the temporal information present in their data. Sallam *et al.* [45] used TPC-C, AuctionMark, Epinions and SEATS. In this paper, they defined the role feature by investigating the purpose and meaning of each transaction in each workload. The different transactions are then grouped to the role of either worker or client. However, there is no exact specification given on the grouping. Sallam and Bertino [41] used SEATS and TPC-C benchmarks and defined each scenario from each workload as an individual role. This approach is reproducible and can be used to compare the different implementation of outlier detection models.

Singh *et al.* [50] used only TPC-C, adding three sensitivity groups (low medium and high) to the tributes. They evaluated their system using precision and recall.

Bu and Cho [10] and Ronao and Cho [39] used TPC-E database benchmark [56] in their experiments. TPC-E simulates the OLTP workload of a brokerage firm. They adopted only the schema of TPC-E and its 12 transaction types as roles to simulate the Role-Based Access Control mechanism. They referenced the database footprint and pseudo-code from the standard specification for the role implementation. The limitation is that there is no available load generator based on TPC-E at the moment. Hence, there might be limitations in terms of reproducibility.

We observe that most works have resorted to generating synthetic datasets or creating one from benchmarks. This could be attributed to the difficulty in obtaining real-life datasets as database logs could contain highly sensitive information. As such, using datasets obtained from running benchmarks is a more viable approach for the work which this paper focuses on. Using datasets from benchmarks provides a way to evaluate and demonstrate the effectiveness of the system. Datasets from benchmark allow experiments to be reproduced. Furthermore, they also simulate environments that are closer to real-life data compared to synthetic data with pre-defined random distributions.

3 Background

3.1 Machine Learning Algorithms

Anomaly detection systems identify intrusion by identifying transactions that deviate from normal usage patterns. Machine learning can be used to learn these normal patterns and to identify anomalies [25], and it has two types: supervised learning and unsupervised learning.

Supervised learning requires labelled data and tries to map data to labels based on the existing data-label pairs in the training data. Role-based Access Control [47], which groups users into roles, is a widely accepted access control model in commercial organisations [51]. As we have seen with DBSAFE, roles can be used as labels, and a machine learning model can learn a mapping of queries to roles. During analysis, whenever a query is classified into a role that is different from the role associated with the query, it is then reported as an anomaly [44].

Unsupervised learning, on the other hand, does not require labelled data during training. The model tries to find patterns from training data without any prior knowledge. After patterns are found, we can mark the data that deviate from learned patterns as anomalies [34]. Cluster analysis [34] and autoencoders [4] are two example tools for the unsupervised learning approach. In this paper, we adopt a supervised machine learning approach and evaluate several classification models: K-Nearest Neighbours, Support Vector Machine, Random Forest and Convolutional Neural Network.

K-Nearest Neighbours. The K-Nearest Neighbours algorithm is a non-parametric algorithm widely used in classification and regression tasks due to its simplicity [2,24]. It is based on the assumption that samples that are close in some distance metric gives similar classification or output values [15]. For classification problems, the basic form of the algorithm is to predict the label of a new sample as the majority label of the K-Nearest samples in the training dataset. In the paper, we used Euclidean distance as the distance metric and chose k according to the size of the dataset.

Support Vector Machine. The support vector machine is a supervised machine learning model originally proposed by Vapnik and Lerner for classification [58], it can also be used for regression tasks [52]. The original algorithm proposed by Vapnik and Lerner [58] is a linear classifier which gives maximal margin for good generalisation. The algorithm is extended to perform non-linear classification using the kernel trick by Boser, Guyon, and Vapnik [8]. The support vector machine was assumed to separate the training data without error, which means training data must be linearly separable on kernel space. To overcome the problem, the soft margin was introduced by Cortes and Vapnik [14] to allow learning with errors.

For classification tasks, SVM is designed to work on two-group classification problems. The multi-class task is often performed by decomposing it into several binary classification problems. Common approaches include "one-against-all", "one-against-one", and directed acyclic graph support vector machine [11].

We choose the linear kernel and "one-against-one" approach based on experimentation with sample data.

Random Forest. Random forest is an ensemble learning method based on multiple decision trees, and it is often used for classification and regression tasks [30]. Its basic component, decision tree, consists of three components which include nodes, branches, and leaves [40]. Each decision node represents an attribute to be tested. Branches connect the nodes and indicate the decision made based on the value of the test attribute. Leaf nodes are the terminal nodes that comprise the class to which an instance belongs. During training, a decision tree is built from the root. At each node, the algorithm chooses the attribute based on which the branches give most information gain. During prediction, the algorithm traverses the tree according to the branch conditions and give the output based on the leaf node selected by the terminal branch condition. Using only one tree to do prediction tends to over-fit the training data, and the random forest algorithm is proposed to overcome this problem [18]. The basic idea of random forest is to construct multiple decision trees based on randomly chosen attributes during training, and select the most popular class as final decision during prediction [9,54].

Artificial Neural Network. The artificial neural network is a machine learning model based on layers of simple, connected processors called neurons [48]. In this model, input neurons receive information from input data while other neurons receive signals from the previous layer of neurons. After receiving the data, each neuron conducts a weighted linear combination of signals, applies a nonlinear activation function to it and outputs the signal to the next layer. The final layer gives the solution to the problem.

Inspired by the observation that extracting local features is used frequently in visual pattern recognition tasks, the convolutional neural network is designed by putting a layer that collects local features in the network, and it demonstrated strong performance for handwritten zip code recognition task [27]. Lu et al. [31] proposed to use the convolutional neural network to detect anomaly in big data system logs and demonstrated promising accuracy.

In this paper, we choose the one-dimensional convolutional neural network as the artificial neural network model.

3.2   Query Embedding

We introduce the problem of query representation as one of the opportunities that we would explore in this paper.

To determine the features to be used by machine learning algorithms, one approach is to use hand-engineered domain-specific features (e.g. quadruplet [44]) while the other approach is to let machine extract features from data automatically. This approach is often referred to as feature learning or representation learning. Representation learning [5] aims to find a dense vector representation of input that captures the relationship between the inputs (e.g., the more similar the vector representation is, the more similar structure the input data has). We would like to apply representation learning to create a feature vector to represent a query.

Jain et al. [22] proposed Query2Vec to learn vector representation of queries. The idea is to convert raw query or query plan to a text token list, and then apply natural language process techniques to learn a representation of the list. They mentioned that literals and constants were removed during the preprocessing steps because the network cannot learn numeric relationships. They also stated that embeddings learned from query plans captured queries' behaviour better than those learned from raw queries. They applied two representation learning methods, namely Doc2Vec [26] and LSTM Autoencoder [29], to linearise the query plan tree and analyse the performance of the embedding layer when used under various circumstances including workload summarisation, classifying queries by error.

We used LSTM Autoencoder to train queries' representation using their execution plans and examined the representation's performance for classification problems using various machine learning methods including K-Nearest Neighbour, Support Vector Machine, Random Forest and Convolutional Neural Network.

3.3   OLTP-Bench Benchmark

We decided to use the OLTP-Bench benchmark as a means to create our dataset. OLTP-Bench benchmark is an open-source tool for benchmarking DBMSs that contain various sets of workloads [16]. Using the OLTP-Bench benchmark, we can generate workloads of the various benchmark that are implemented as well as adjust the duration, rate, and weights of the workloads' transactions.

There are several benchmarks in the framework and they are categorised into three classes: transactional, web-oriented and feature testing [16]. We only consider the transactional benchmarks as datasets for our experiment as it is only possible to include information on the role used in those transaction benchmarks. In our experiments, we use the OLTP-Bench benchmark to create our synthetic datasets which allows for our research to be reproducible. We further elaborate on the list of benchmarks that are provided by the OLTP-Bench benchmark.

AuctionMark. It simulates the activities in an auction house [3]. The benchmark consists of 13 tables and 9 transaction types. There are two main user types in the system: buyer and seller. The transaction types are: (1) Get Item, (2) Get User Info, (3) New Bid, (4) New Comment, (5) New Comment Response, (6) New Feedback, (7) New Purchase, (8) New Item, and (9) Update Item.

CH-benCHmark. This is a modified version of a combined workload of TPC-C [55] and TPC-H [13]. It consists of both OLTP and OLAP transactions so it is suitable to evaluate database management systems that handle both types of transactions. The resulting benchmark contains twelve tables in total, three of them only used by TPC-C, six of them used by both TPC-C and TPC-H that are the result of extending existing tables used by TPC-C, and three of them exclusively used by TPC-H. CH-benCHmark contains the five OLTP queries from TPC-C, as well as 22 modified OLAP queries from TPC-H. The transaction types are: (1) Payment, (2) New Order, (3) Order Status, (4) Stock Level, (5) Delivery and (6) Analyst.

SEATS. It models the activity of airline ticketing systems [53]. The benchmark consists of eight tables and six transaction types. The six transactions types are: (1) Find Flights, (2) Find Open Seats, (3) Update Customer, (4) New Reservation, (5) Update Reservation and (6) Delete Reservation. In our experiment, transactions that are rollbacked are removed for simplicity.

SmallBank. It simulates the activity of a banking application doing simple banking transactions [1]. The benchmark consists of three tables and six transaction types. The benchmark is created to simulate the activity of a customer having a checking and savings account. In the original paper, there are only five transaction types but in OLTP-Bench benchmark, Send Payment is added to transfer funds between the two accounts. The six transaction types are (1) Amalgamate, (2) Balance, (3) Deposit Checking, (4) Send Payment, (5) Transact Savings, (6) and Write Check.

TATP. This benchmark simulates the activity of a typical telecommunication application [37]. It simulates a database that contains information about subscribers, phone numbers, services subscribed, access privileges and location of subscriber's handset. The benchmark consists of four tables and seven transaction types. The seven transaction types are (1) Get User Info, (2) Remove Call Forwarding, (3) User Update, (4) Get Number, (5) Get User Data, (6) Call Forwarding and (7) Location Update.

TPC-C. It simulates the activities of a wholesale supplier [55]. The benchmark consists of nine tables and five transaction types. The five transaction types are (1) Payment, (2) New Order, (3) Order Status, (4) Stock Level and (5) Delivery.

The advantage of using the OLTP-Bench benchmark is that the implementation of the workload is publicly available and there are various benchmarks built-in as part of the projects. Hence, this makes the dataset used reproducible and easily configurable for different needs.

4   Approach

We outline our approach which replaces the Naïve Bayes classifier of DBSAFE by different machine learning algorithms and data representation. We also add a query embedding mechanism called Query2Vec to improve the feature representation.

4.1   Role-Based Anomaly Detection: DBSAFE

Sallam *et al.* [44] devise a role-based anomaly detection system called DBSAFE. They begin by creating a data representation for each query using a quadruplet that consists of the type of the query, a Boolean representation of the tables accessed, a list of Boolean representation of the column accessed per table, and selectivity of query which is a list of the number of rows affected per tables.

For creating the quadruplet, we begin by following the way they use the PostgreSQL's optimiser, to get a query plan in the form of an execution tree. We first query the list of tables and columns from the database to be able to create a dictionary linking each of those columns and tables to the index of the bit representing it inside the quadruplet. For queries that we received, we get the type of the query (SELECT, UPDATE, DELETE, INSERT). We use the EXPLAIN function to get the execution tree for the query in JSON format. By going through this tree in post-order, we can compute the selectivity as well as the tables and columns accessed, which we use to generate the quadruplet.

Role profiles are then constructed using quadruplets and the anomaly detection mechanism is essentially a classification problem. They tested the profiles using two classifiers: Binary and Naïve Bayes classifier. The paper concludes that Naïve Bayes classifier performs better than Binary classifier.

The Naïve Bayes classifier used by DBSAFE computes the probability of the query being submitted by users of each known roles by using the information inside the quadruplet. The role classification is decided using the Maximum-A-Posteriori decision rule which returns the role with the highest probability of doing this query. The result of the classification is then compared to the actual role of the person querying. The query is classified as an anomaly if the role is a mismatch.

4.2   Machine Learning and Data Representation

We propose to evaluate whether other machine learning algorithms can be used in place of DBSAFE's Naïve Bayes and we experiment with four machine learning algorithms: K-Nearest Neighbours, Support Vector Machine, Random Forest and Convolutional Neural Network. The four machine learning algorithms are chosen to cover a variety of supervised learning techniques such as neural network, ensemble, support vector machine and nearest neighbours to better assess the accuracy the different techniques for the different datasets.

As we are using the machine learning algorithms from scikit-learn library, the input to the functions are matrices, hence it does not support the nested data format of the quadruplet. This, in turn, requires us to modify the quadruplet's structure to make the data usable by those algorithms. In that effect, we modify the quadruplet by flattening the nested array and removing the table access binary array. The details of the modification is elaborated in the experimental setup.

4.3   Query2Vec Implementation

The quadruplet is not a suitable input format for the machine learning algorithms that we have selected. We look for embedding techniques that can represent the structure of queries in a flat feature vector. One such technique is Query2Vec. We explain how we use Query2Vec to generate vector representation for queries.

We first build a representation vector of query plan tokens using LSTM autoencoder. Since the query plan is tree-structured, we need to linearise the query plan before extracting tokens. Instead of in-order traversal mentioned in the paper [22], we chose post-order traversal to go through the execution tree. This traversal order is the same order DBSAFE [44] used to process the execution tree. Furthermore, when a linearised query plan is long, it may need cutting to fit into the LSTM model. By using post-order traversal, the query plan which is most related to the output is kept when pre-truncating is applied. During the tokenisation step, literals and constants are removed because the network is not able to learn numeric relationships. Since brackets and comma appear many times and can greatly increase the sequence length, they are also removed from token lists. During representation learning step, we apply pre-padding for short token lists and pre-truncating for long lists. The max sequence length is determined by both sequence length distribution and hardware capability. When training is finished, we extract the trained LSTM autoencoder's encoding part and use it to generate query embeddings.

To test the performance of representation vectors, we use them as features and apply the machine learning algorithms to perform classification tasks. We assess the accuracy of different algorithms using extended CH-benCHmark dataset in Sect. 5.7.

5   Comparative Empirical Performance Evaluation

In the following experiments, the workloads from OLTP-bench are all run against a PostgreSQL V.12 databases to be able to use the latest stable version of PostgreSQL's optimiser. Both the PostgreSQL database, the quadruplet builder and the OLTP-bench are run in Docker containers by using Docker Desktop version 2.2.03 with the Docker engine version 19.03.5 and compose version 1.25.4.

For machine learning algorithms, the machine learning algorithm's implementations come from two packages: Tensorflow and Scikit-learn.

5.1   Dataset

OLTP-Bench benchmark has been used in several publications across different experimental conditions making it a suitable benchmarking tool for our work. However, one limitation of OLTP-Bench benchmark is the lack of information on the role used for most of the benchmarks. As such, we need to define roles for the transactions in the benchmarks for it to be effectively used in our experiment. There are two approaches to how roles can be introduced.

The first approach is to use OLTP-Bench benchmark and define the roles as each transaction in the benchmarks. We label this dataset as OLTP-Bench benchmark dataset. The second approach is to use CH-benCHmark, which is a combined TPC-C and TPC-H benchmark and extend CH-benCHmark by defining meaningful roles from the list of transactions. This dataset labelled as the extended CH-benchmark dataset.

OLTP-Bench Benchmark Dataset. In the OLTP-Bench benchmark dataset, we define the role of the users as the individual transaction type within the benchmark. For example, TPC-C contains five transaction types and therefore, each of the transactions are considered as one role so there are five roles. For the case of CH-benCHmark used in this dataset, the twenty tow TPC-H queries [57] considered as one role in OLTP-Bench benchmark dataset. Hence, there are six roles: five from TPC-C and one from TPC-H. In generating the workload for OLTP-Bench benchmark dataset, we use the default parameters given in the OLTP-Bench benchmark.

There are several limitations to the first approach. The first limitation is that in some benchmarks, after closer inspection of the queries for each transaction, we can see that there are some similarities or intended cluster among the transactions. Hence, the role definitions are not meaningful. This leads to confusion for the model to classify such transactions. Another limitation is that such definition of roles, where roles are strictly restricted to do one transaction, is unlikely in real life. Therefore, we have decided to explore another dataset where the transactions are grouped meaningfully.

Extended CH-benCHmark Dataset. In the second approach, we created the extended CH-benCHmark to address the limitations of the first approach. In the extended CH-benCHmark, we have studied the transaction types of the original CH-benCHmark as well as look into the queries and table access in order to assign meaningful roles to each of the transaction types. Table 1 describe the assignment of roles to each transaction types.

Table 1. Extended CH-benCHmark roles.

Role	Transaction/Query	Type
(1) Warehouse	Order Status, Delivery, Stock Level	OLTP
(2) Customer	New Order, Payment	
(3) Business	Query 1, 6, 11, 12, 15, 17, 21, 22	OLAP
(4) Management	Query 5, 7, 8, 9	
(5) Logistics	Query 2, 3, 4, 16	
(6) Marketing	Query 10, 13, 14, 18, 19, 20	

CH-benCHmark is a modified version of the combined workload between TPC-C and TPC-H. TPC-C is an Online Transaction Processing (OLTP) system which generally consists of several queries grouped as transactions while TPC-H is an Online Analytical Processing (OLAP) system that consists of individual queries.

The five OLTP transaction types from TPC-C are divided into two roles which are warehouse and customer. We have determined that Order Status, Delivery and Stock Level are transactions that are likely submitted by (1) Warehouse employees who are coordinating warehouse operations while a (2) Customer is purchasing items through New Order and Payment transactions. Meanwhile, the 22 modified OLAP queries from TPC-H are divided to four roles: the (3) Business team who look into aggregate sales, revenue and order information from customers, the (4) Management team who analyse sales and revenue information in a global-level across different regions, the (5) Logistics teams who query information about shipments and logistics, and the (6) Marketing team who analyse information for promotions and campaigns.

5.2   Machine Learning

For the machine learning algorithms, we use the scikit-learn's implementation of KNeighborsClassifier for K-Nearest Neighbours, SVC for Support Vector Machine and RandomForestClassifier for Random Forest. For Convolutional Neural Network, we built LeNet [28] architecture using Keras. We compare the performance of these algorithms with Naïve Bayes classifier from DBSAFE.

The parameters of the machine learning algorithms are generally set at default and we set a random state for our experiments where it is possible such as Random Forest and Support Vector Machine. For KNeighborsClassifier, we set $n\_neighbours = 5$. For SVC, we set the $kernel = $ 'linear' as our experiments has shown that they perform better than 'rbf' for our datasets, and we set $gamma = $ 'scale'. For RandomForestClassifier, the $n\_estimators = 100$.

In DBSAFE, the proportion of roles are equal as their calculation depends on the role probability. Since we are comparing our results with DBSAFE's, we use the same approach. For all experiments, we first re-sample the dataset to ensure that the distribution of queries across all roles is equal. The queries are re-sampled to 10,000 queries and equally divided across the number of roles depending on the benchmark. Furthermore, to ensure consistency and robust results, we run a k-fold cross-validation using scikit-learn StratifiedKFold with $n\_splits = 5$ and $shuffle = $ False. The metrics that we use to evaluate the performance are the accuracy and confusion matrix.

We describe the feature extraction method for our experiments. For DBSAFE' Naïve Bayes, the input is a quadruplet following the model of [44]. The inputs to the other machine learning algorithms in Sect. 5.3 to 5.6 use the features extracted from the quadruplet. Section 5.7 and 5.8 use features extracted using Query2Vec.

Feature Extraction from Quadruplet. The features include four parts based on quadruplets [44]. The first feature is command type which includes "SELECT", "INSERT", "UPDATE" and "DELETE". The second feature is the list of tables affected. The third feature is the list of columns affected. The last feature is selectivity which is the number of rows affected for all tables. All the data are obtained from PostgreSQL optimiser. Since the first three sets of features are categorical, we use one-hot encoding for pre-processing. The final format of our input data is: 1 column of SQL command, $m * n$ columns of attribute access per table where m is the number of attributes in a table and n is the number of table in the database, n columns of the selectivity for each table.

Feature Extraction Using Query2Vec. The features described above in the quadruplet are obtained using PostgresSQL optimiser. Similarly, we use PostgreSQL to obtain the query plan for each query. The query plans are then tokenised and passed to Query2Vec to generate vector representation of the tokens. The length of the vector is 100. Subsequently, these vectors are used as feature vectors for the classification task.

The experimental results are organised in the following manner. We test the machine learning algorithms on OLTP-Bench benchmark dataset and extended CH-benCHmark dataset. Section 5.3 and 5.4 are experiments using OLTP-Bench benchmark dataset with feature extraction from the quadruplet. Section 5.5 and 5.6 are experiments using extended CH-benCHmark dataset with feature extraction from the quadruplet. Section 5.7 and 5.8 are experiments using extended CH-benCHmark dataset with feature extraction from Query2Vec.

5.3   Experimental Results: OLTP-Bench Benchmark Dataset

There are six benchmarks within the OLTP-Bench benchmark Dataset: Auctionmark, CH-benCHmark, SEATS, Smallbank, TATP and TPCC. We train and test K-Nearest Neighbours, Support Vector Machine, Random Forest, Convolutional Neural Network and DBSAFE's Naïve Bayes based on the 5-fold cross-validation. For each experiment, the result are presented using a confusion matrix with accuracy for each role and also overall accuracy.

We first show the results of the individual benchmark for each machine learning algorithm. The accuracy results for each machine learning algorithm are shown in Tables 2, 3, 4, 5, 7 and 8.

K-Nearest Neighbours. We start by running K-Nearest Neighbours (KNN) on the various benchmarks in the OLTP-Bench benchmark. Figure 1b shows the 5-fold confusion matrix and Table 2 shows the accuracy for AuctionMark dataset. KNN achieves an overall 74.21% accuracy. It can be observed that KNN achieves 100% accuracy for New Comment Response and it achieves around 90% accuracy in three other roles: Get User Info, New Item and Update Item. New Bid, New Feedback and New Purchase achieve an accuracy in the range of 60% to 70%. However, Get Item and New Comment only achieve an accuracy of 45.9% and 52% respectively. Get Item and Get User Info are often confused with one another, while for the rest, the roles are misclassified to either New Comment Response, New Purchase and Update Item.

Figure 2b shows the 5-fold confusion matrix and Table 3 shows the accuracy for CH-benCHmark. KNN' overall accuracy is at 88.19%. It achieves greater than 75% for all the roles in CH-benCHmark. It achieves 100% accuracy for Stock Level queries followed by New Order and Analyst at 96.46% and 92.44% respectively. Order Status, Delivery and Payment follow with 87.03%, 78.09% and 75.33% respectively. There is misclassification among Payment, Order Status and Delivery. Some queries from New Order are misclassified to Payment and Stock Level while some queries of Analyst are misclassified to Stock Level and Delivery.

Figure 3b shows the 5-fold confusion matrix and Table 4 shows the accuracy for SEATS. For SEATS dataset, the overall accuracy is 82.98%. The performance varies across different roles with Find Flights and Update Reservation achieving 100% accuracy. It is followed by Find Open Seats and Update Customer at 99.46% and 84.81%. Delete Reservation achieves 61.82% accuracy while New Reservation achieves 51.98% accuracy. There is often misclassification among New Reservation, Update Customer and Delete Reservation and on top of the confusion between the three, Update Customer also misclassified a quarter of its queries to Update Reservation.

Figure 4b shows the 5-fold confusion matrix and Table 5 shows the accuracy for SmallBank. SmallBank achieves an overall accuracy of 33.84%. Send Payment has the highest accuracy at 69.87% while the remaining roles have accuracy less than 36%. KNN cannot differentiate among the roles as the misclassification happens almost across all roles. Amalgamate, Balance and Write Check have their queries misclassified to all other roles while Send Payment and Transact Savings have their queries misclassified to four other roles.

Figure 5b shows the 5-fold confusion matrix and Table 7 shows the accuracy for TATP. For TATP, the overall accuracy is 85.77%. KNN achieves 100% accuracy for Get User Info, Get Number, Get User Data and Call Forwarding while Remove Call Forwarding and User Update are at 90.48% and 70.38% respectively. Queries that are largely misclassified are from Location Update with only 39.78% accuracy. The queries in Remove Call Forwarding and User Update are misclassified to Location Update while Location Update queries are confused with Remove Call Forwarding and User Update.

Figure 6b shows the 5-fold confusion matrix and Table 8 shows the accuracy for TPC-C. For TPC-C, the overall accuracy is 89.02%. Stock Level achieves 100% accuracy while New Order has 95.05% accuracy. The remaining ones: Order Status, Delivery and Payment are at 87.15%, 83.8% and 79.6%. There is misclassification among Payment, Order Status and Delivery while New Order is sometimes confused with either Payment or Stock Level.

Support Vector Machine. We run Support Vector Machine (SVM) on OLTP-Bench benchmark dataset and the confusion matrices are as follows.

Figure 1c shows the 5-fold confusion matrix and Table 2 shows the accuracy for AuctionMark. SVM achieves an overall 75.17% accuracy. The performance of SVM for AuctionMark dataset varies widely. It achieves 100% accuracy for

New Comment Response and Update Item. Get User Info and New Item achieve accuracy of 94.15% and 91.18% respectively. New Bid, New Feedback and New Purchase achieve accuracy between 60% to 70%. However, Get Item and New Comment only achieve an accuracy of 45.9% and 52% respectively. There is confusion between Get Item and Get User Info. Out of the remaining seven roles, four of them misclassified their roles to New Comment Response and Update Item.

Figure 2c shows the 5-fold confusion matrix and Table 3 shows the accuracy for CH-benCHmark. SVM has an overall accuracy of 90.07%. It achieves 100% accuracy for Stock Level and Order Status queries followed by New Order at 96.46%. Both Payment and Analyst achieve an average accuracy of 86% while the lowest is Delivery at 71.91%. The misclassified roles are generally misclassified to two other different roles.

Figure 3c shows the 5-fold confusion matrix and Table 4 shows the accuracy for SEATS. For SEATS dataset, the overall accuracy is 84.9%. The performance varies across different roles with Find Flights and Update Reservation achieving 100% accuracy. It is followed by Find Open Seats, Delete Reservation and Update Reservation at 99.46%, 97.54% and 75.51%. However, New Reservation only achieves 37.09% accuracy where it is misclassified to three other roles. There is also misclassification between Update Customer and Delete Reservation.

Figure 4c shows the 5-fold confusion matrix and Table 5 shows the accuracy for SmallBank. It has higher accuracy than KNN with an overall accuracy of 39.72%. Send Payment has 100% accuracy but Amalgamate and Write Check achieve 0% accuracy meaning SVM completely misclassified these roles. The remaining roles have accuracy of around 40% to 50%. There is less confusion across the roles compared to KNN but misclassification still happens across Balance, Deposit Checking and Transact Savings.

Figure 5c shows the 5-fold confusion matrix and Table 7 shows the accuracy for TATP. For TATP dataset, the overall accuracy using SVM is 85.74%. It achieves 100% accuracy for Get User Info, Get Number, Get User Data and Call Forwarding while Location Update and User Update are at 79.34% and 70.17% respectively. However, Remove Call Forwarding has lower accuracy of 50.91%. The queries in Remove Call Forwarding and User Update are misclassified to Location Update while Location Update queries are confused with User Update.

Figure 6c shows the 5-fold confusion matrix and Table 8 shows the accuracy for TPC-C. For TPC-C dataset, the overall accuracy is 90.22%. Both Order Status and Stock Level achieve 100% accuracy while New Order has an accuracy of 95.05%. The remaining ones are Delivery and Payment at 82.55% and 73.5%. There is misclassification among Payment, Order Status and Delivery while New Order is sometimes confused with either Payment or Stock Level.

Random Forest. We run Random Forest on OLTP-Bench benchmark dataset and the confusion matrices are as follows. All confusion matrices for Random Forest are the same as SVM except for SEATS dataset.

Figure 1d shows the 5-fold confusion matrix and Table 2 shows the accuracy for AuctionMark dataset. For AuctionMark dataset, the results for Random Forest are the same as SVM with an overall accuracy of 75.17%. The performance of Random Forest for AuctionMark dataset varies widely. It can be observed that it achieves 100% accuracy for New Comment Response and Update Item. Get User Info and New Item achieve accuracy of 94.15% and 91.18% respectively. New Bid, New Feedback and New Purchase achieve accuracy between 60% to 70%. However, Get Item and New Comment only achieve an accuracy of 45.9% and 52% respectively. There is confusion between Get Item and Get User Info. Out of the remaining seven roles, four of them misclassified their roles to New Comment Response and Update Item.

Figure 2d shows the 5-fold confusion matrix and Table 3 shows the accuracy for CH-benCHmark. The overall accuracy is 90.07%. Random Forest achieves greater than 70% for all the roles in CH-benCHmark. The results for Random Forest is the same as SVM. It achieves 100% accuracy for Stock Level and Order Status queries followed by New Order at 96.46%. Both Payment and Analyst achieve an average accuracy of 86% while the lowest is Delivery at 71.91%. The misclassified roles are generally misclassified to two other roles.

Figure 3d shows the 5-fold confusion matrix and Table 4 shows the accuracy for SEATS. For SEATS dataset, the overall accuracy is 84.9%. The performance varies across different roles with Find Flights and Update Reservation achieving 100% accuracy. It is followed by Find Open Seats, Delete Reservation and Update Customer at 99.46%, 97.54% and 75.51%. However, New Reservation only achieves 37.09% accuracy where it is misclassified to three other roles.

Figure 4d shows the 5-fold confusion matrix and Table 5 shows the accuracy for SmallBank. For SmallBank dataset, the results for Random Forest are rather similar to SVM with an overall accuracy of 39.76%. Send Payment has 100% accuracy but Amalgamate and Write Check achieve 0% accuracy meaning SVM completely misclassified these roles. The remaining roles have accuracy of around 30% to 60%. There is less confusion across the roles compared to KNN but misclassification still happens across Balance, Deposit Checking and Transact Savings. No role that is classified as Amalgamate and Write Check.

Figure 5d shows the 5-fold confusion matrix and Table 7 shows the accuracy for TATP. The overall accuracy is 85.74%. For TATP dataset, Random Forest performs the same as SVM where it achieves 100% accuracy for Get User Info, Get Number, Get User Data and Call Forwarding while Location Update and User Update are at 79.34% and 70.17% respectively. However, Remove Call Forwarding only achieves an accuracy of 50.91%. The queries in Remove Call Forwarding and User Update are misclassified to Location Update while Location Update queries are confused with User Update.

Figure 6d shows the 5-fold confusion matrix and Table 8 shows the accuracy for TPC-C. The overall accuracy is 90.22%. For TPC-C dataset, Random Forest has the same result as SVM. Both Order Status and Stock Level achieve 100% accuracy while New Order is classified with an accuracy of 95.05%. The remaining ones are Delivery and Payment at 82.55% and 73.5%. There is misclassification among Payment, Order Status and Delivery while New Order is sometimes confused with either Payment or Stock Level. There is confusion among Payment, Order Status and Delivery while New Order is misclassified to Payment and Stock Level.

Convolutional Neural Network. We run Convolutional Neural Network (CNN) on OLTP-Bench benchmark dataset and the confusion matrices are as follows.

Figure 1e shows the 5-fold confusion matrix and Table 2 shows the accuracy for AuctionMark dataset. The Convolutional Neural Network achieves an overall 75.17% accuracy. For AuctionMark dataset, the results for CNN are the same as SVM and Random Forest. It can be observed that CNN achieves 100% accuracy for New Comment Response and Update Item followed by Get User Info and New Item at 94.15% and 91.18% respectively. New Bid, New Feedback and New Purchase where it achieves accuracy between 60% to 70%. However, Get Item and New Comment achieves accuracy of 45.9% and 52% respectively.

Figure 2e shows the 5-fold confusion matrix and Table 3 shows the accuracy for CH-benCHmark. The overall accuracy is 89.72%. CNN achieves greater than 70% for all the roles. It achieves 100% accuracy for Stock Level and Order Status queries followed by New Order at 96.46%. Both Payment and Analyst achieve accuracy ranging from 80% to 90% while the lowest is Delivery at 71.73%.

Figure 3e shows the 5-fold confusion matrix and Table 4 shows the accuracy for SEATS. For SEATS dataset, CNN, the overall accuracy is 86.19%. Find Flights and Update Reservation achieve 100% accuracy while Find Open Seats is close to perfect at 99.46%. The accuracy of Delete Reservation and Update Reservation is around 85%. However, New Reservation has 37.09% accuracy where it is misclassified to three other roles.

Figure 4e shows the 5-fold confusion matrix and Table 5 shows the accuracy for SmallBank. For SmallBank dataset, CNN achieves an overall accuracy of 39.62%. Send Payment has 100% accuracy while Write Check and Amalgamate achieve 0% and 7.08%accuracy. The remaining roles have accuracy of around 30% to 60%. There is less confusion across the roles compared to KNN but misclassification still happens across Balance, Deposit Checking and Transact Savings.

Figure 5e shows the 5-fold confusion matrix and Table 7 shows the accuracy for TATP. The overall accuracy is 85.84%. It achieves 100% accuracy for Get User Info, Get Number, Get User Data and Call Forwarding while Remove Call Forwarding and Location Update achieve around 70% accuracy. The queries in Remove Call Forwarding and User Update are misclassified to Location Update while Location Update queries are confused with User Update.

Figure 6e shows the 5-fold confusion matrix and Table 8 shows the accuracy for TPC-C. For TPC-C dataset, CNN has an accuracy of 90.21%. Both Order Status and Stock Level achieve 100% accuracy while New Order is close to perfect at 95.05%. The remaining ones are Delivery and Payment at 79.75% and

76.25%. There is misclassification among Payment, Order Status and Delivery while New Order is sometimes confused with either Payment or Stock Level.

DBSAFE's Naïve Bayes Classifier. Lastly, we run DBSAFE's Naïve Bayes classifier on OLTP-Bench benchmark dataset as a baseline comparison and the confusion matrices are as follows.

Figure 1a shows the 5-fold confusion matrix and Table 2 shows the accuracy for AuctionMark dataset. For AuctionMark dataset, the results for DBSAFE are worse from the other Machine Learning algorithms. The overall accuracy is lower at 71.86% compared to others at 75.16%. DBSAFE performs worse for Get User Info, New Item and New Purchase while it performs better only for Get Item. The rest of the roles have the same accuracy.

Figure 2a shows the 5-fold confusion matrix and Table 3 shows the accuracy for CH-benCHmark. For Ch-benCHmark, The overall accuracy is 87.04%. It achieves 100% accuracy for Stock Level and Order Status queries followed by New Order at 96.46%. Both Payment and Analyst achieve accuracy ranging from 80% to 85% while the lowest is Delivery at 57.80%.

Figure 3a shows the 5-fold confusion matrix and Table 4 shows the accuracy for SEATS. The overall accuracy is 84.39%. Find Flights and Update Reservation achieve 100% accuracy while Find Open Seats is close to perfect at 99.46%. The accuracy of Delete Reservation and Update Reservation is around 85%. However, New Reservation only achieves 37.09% accuracy where it is misclassified to three other roles.

Figure 4a shows the 5-fold confusion matrix and Table 5 shows the accuracy for SmallBank. For SmallBank dataset, the overall accuracy is 30.52%. Amalgamate and Balance achieves 0% accuracy which is different from the other machine learning model. Transact Savings achieves higher accuracy at 68.01% while the remaining roles have accuracy around 20% to 40%.

Figure 5a shows the 5-fold confusion matrix and Table 7 shows the accuracy for TATP. The overall accuracy is 85.95%. For TATP dataset, DBSAFE predicted one more role with 100% accuracy but another role suffers as a result. It achieves 100% accuracy for Get User Info, Get Number, Get User Data, Call Forwarding and Location Update while both Remove Call Forwarding and User Update achieve around 51% accuracy, with all the misclassification being queries misclassified as queries from Location Update.

Figure 6a shows the 5-fold confusion matrix and Table 8 shows the accuracy for TPC-C. The overall accuracy is high at 90.27%. Both Order Status and Stock Level achieve 100% accuracy while New Order is close to perfect at 95.05%. The remaining ones are Payment and Delivery at 85.10% and 71.20%. There is misclassification between Payment and Order Status while New Order is sometimes confused with either Payment or Stock Level.

After showing all the confusion matrices for each machine learning algorithm and each benchmark, we compare the performance among the algorithms and analyse the results.

5.4   Comparative Analysis: OLTP-Bench Benchmark Dataset

We have tested the four machine learning algorithms across the six different benchmarks within OLTP-Bench benchmark. We compare the results for each dataset for the different machine learning algorithms. Figures 1 to 6 show the confusion matrices for each benchmark for each algorithm.

AuctionMark. For AuctionMark, the algorithms achieve an accuracy of around 70% to 75% as seen in Table 2. SVM, Random Forest and CNN have the same accuracy. KNN has similar accuracy but it is slightly lower as it performs slightly worse for one role. The overall accuracy of the four machine learning algorithms still outperform DBSAFE Naïve Bayes.

Table 2. Comparison of 5-fold CV accuracy for AuctionMark dataset.

Roles/Algorithms	KNN	SVM	RF	CNN	DBSAFE
1	45.90%	45.90%	45.90%	45.90%	47.25%
2	94.15%	94.15%	94.15%	94.15%	81.82%
3	65.35%	65.35%	65.35%	65.35%	65.35%
4	52.03%	52.03%	52.03%	52.03%	52.03%
5	100.0%	100.0%	100.0%	100.0%	100.0%
6	67.87%	67.87%	67.87%	67.87%	67.87%
7	91.00%	91.18%	91.18%	91.09%	83.26%
8	62.65%	60.13%	60.13%	60.13%	49.23%
9	89.02%	100.0%	100.0%	100.0%	100.0%
Total	74.21%	75.17%	75.17%	75.16%	71.86%

1: Get Item. 2: Get User Info. 3: New Bid. 4: New Comment. 5: New Comment Response.
6: New Feedback. 7: New Item. 8: New Purchase. 9: Update Item

We can see that for this benchmark, SVM, RF and CNN end up with the same classification in Fig. 1. KNN and DBSAFE also seem to perform the same type of misclassification as the other three algorithms, but they are less accurate with KNN sometimes misclassifying Update Item as New Purchase, and DBSAFE being less accurate than the other algorithms in classifying Get User Info and New Item queries. Overall, these algorithms have difficulty classifying Get Item where they are misclassified to Get User Info. We also have an overall lower accuracy for New Comment compared to the other roles.

The misclassification of the Get Item as Get User Info could be explained by the fact that the getItem query, which is one of the two queries submitted by Get Item, is similar to the getSellerItems query from Get User Info. Concerning the lower accuracy for New Comment, we can see that the updateUser query, one of the four queries from the New Comment role, is also submitted by users with the New Comment Response role. The updateItemComments query could be confused with the updateItem query from the Update Item role. In general roles like New Comment, New Feedback and New Purchase, which have a query that updates a user account, seems to have part of their overall queries misclassified to New Comment Response. The same thing applies for New Bid and New Purchase that have queries that update an item where their queries are misclassified to Update Item.

CH-benCHmark. For CH-benCHmark the algorithms achieve an accuracy of around 88% as seen in Table 3. SVM and Random Forest have the same accuracy, which is the highest at 90.07% followed by CNN and KNN at 89.72% and 88.19%. The overall accuracies of the four machine learning algorithms still outperform DBSAFE Naïve Bayes which achieves a slightly lower accuracy score of 87.04%.

[DBSAFE]

Roles	1	2	3	4	5	6	7	8	9
1	525	586	0	0	0	0	0	0	0
2	202	909	0	0	0	0	0	0	0
3	179	0	726	0	0	0	5	0	201
4	0	0	0	578	275	0	0	0	258
5	0	0	0	0	1111	0	0	0	0
6	0	0	0	0	357	754	0	0	0
7	0	0	0	88	79	0	925	0	19
8	0	0	121	0	310	0	0	547	133
9	0	0	0	0	0	0	0	0	1111

[KNN]

Roles	1	2	3	4	5	6	7	8	9
1	510	601	0	0	0	0	0	0	0
2	64	1046	0	0	0	0	0	1	0
3	179	0	726	0	0	0	5	38	163
4	0	0	0	578	275	0	0	54	204
5	0	0	0	0	1111	0	0	0	0
6	0	0	0	0	357	754	0	0	0
7	2	0	0	0	79	0	1011	3	16
8	0	0	0	0	310	0	0	696	105
9	0	0	0	0	0	0	0	122	989

[SVM]

Roles	1	2	3	4	5	6	7	8	9
1	510	601	0	0	0	0	0	0	0
2	64	1046	0	1	0	0	0	0	0
3	179	0	726	0	0	0	5	0	201
4	0	0	0	578	275	0	0	0	258
5	0	0	0	0	1111	0	0	0	0
6	0	0	0	0	357	754	0	0	0
7	0	0	0	0	79	0	1013	0	19
8	0	0	0	0	310	0	0	668	133
9	0	0	0	0	0	0	0	0	1111

[RF]

Roles	1	2	3	4	5	6	7	8	9
1	510	601	0	0	0	0	0	0	0
2	64	1046	0	0	0	0	1	0	0
3	179	0	726	0	0	0	5	0	201
4	0	0	0	578	275	0	0	0	258
5	0	0	0	0	1111	0	0	0	0
6	0	0	0	0	357	754	0	0	0
7	0	0	0	0	79	0	1013	0	19
8	0	0	0	0	310	0	0	668	133
9	0	0	0	0	0	0	0	0	1111

[CNN]

Roles	1	2	3	4	5	6	7	8	9
1	510	601	0	0	0	0	0	0	0
2	64	1046	0	0	1	0	0	0	0
3	179	0	726	0	0	0	5	0	201
4	0	0	0	578	275	0	0	0	258
5	0	0	0	0	1111	0	0	0	0
6	0	0	0	0	357	754	0	0	0
7	0	1	0	0	79	0	1012	0	19
8	0	0	0	0	310	0	0	668	133
9	0	0	0	0	0	0	0	0	1111

1: Get Item. 2: Get User Info. 3: New Bid. 4: New Comment. 5: New Comment Response. 6: New Feedback. 7: New Item. 8: New Purchase. 9: Update Item

Fig. 1. AuctionMark's confusion matrices.

We can see for this benchmark in Fig. 2 that the misclassification of 235 queries from Payment as queries from Order Status is consistent across each algorithm. For KNN and CNN, there is misclassification between Payment and Delivery. We can also see that across the machine learning algorithms there are misclassification from New Order and Analyst to Stock level. Another misclassification that appears across all algorithms is from Delivery to Payment or Order Status.

Table 3. Comparison of 5-fold CV accuracy for CH-benCHmark dataset.

Roles/Algorithms	KNN	SVM	RF	CNN	DBSAFE
1	75.33%	85.89%	85.89%	82.11%	85.89%
2	96.46%	96.46%	96.46%	96.46%	94.60%
3	87.03%	100.0%	100.0%	100.0%	100.0%
4	100.0%	100.0%	100.0%	100.0%	100.0%
5	78.09%	71.91%	71.91%	71.73%	57.80%
6	92.44%	86.37%	86.37%	88.24%	84.15%
Total	88.19%	90.07%	90.07%	89.72%	87.04%

1: Payment. 2: New Order. 3: Order Status. 4: Stock Level. 5: Delivery. 6: Analyst

We can also see that some queries from Analyst are misclassified to either Stock Level or Delivery for all machine learning algorithms, except for DBSAFE's

[DBSAFE]

Roles	1	2	3	4	5	6
1	1431	0	235	0	0	0
2	28	1576	0	31	0	31
3	0	0	1666	0	0	0
4	0	0	0	1666	0	0
5	241	0	227	0	963	235
6	0	0	204	60	0	1402

[KNN]

Roles	1	2	3	4	5	6
1	1255	0	235	0	176	0
2	28	1607	0	31	0	0
3	0	0	1450	0	216	0
4	0	0	0	1666	0	0
5	94	0	131	0	1301	140
6	0	0	0	60	66	1540

[SVM]

Roles	1	2	3	4	5	6
1	1431	0	235	0	0	0
2	28	1607	0	31	0	0
3	0	0	1666	0	0	0
4	0	0	0	1666	0	0
5	241	0	227	0	1198	0
6	0	0	0	60	167	1439

[RF]

Roles	1	2	3	4	5	6
1	1431	0	235	0	0	0
2	28	1607	0	31	0	0
3	0	0	1666	0	0	0
4	0	0	0	1666	0	0
5	241	0	227	0	1198	0
6	0	0	0	60	167	1439

[CNN]

Roles	1	2	3	4	5	6
1	1368	0	235	0	63	0
2	28	1607	0	31	0	0
3	0	0	1666	0	0	0
4	0	0	0	1666	0	0
5	196	0	227	0	1195	48
6	0	0	0	60	136	1470

1: Payment. 2: New Order. 3: Order Status. 4: Stock Level. 5: Delivery. 6: Analyst

Fig. 2. CH-Benchmark confusion matrices.

Naïve Bayes where it misclassifies to Order Status and Stock Level instead. We can note that the number of queries from Analyst that are misclassified to Stock Level is consistent across all machine learning algorithms.

Finally, for all machine learning algorithms except for SVM, we have queries from Delivery misclassified as queries from Analysis. The misclassification of queries from Payment as queries from Order Status might come from the fact that both the Payment and Order Status do the customerByNameSQL query. Concerning the confusion between Delivery and Payment, it might come from the fact that both roles have a query that updates the information on a customer. As for the confusion between Delivery and Order Status, it comes from the ordStatGetNewestOrdSQL which is confused with the delivSumOrderAmountSQL query from delivery.

SEATS. For SEATS, the algorithms achieve an accuracy of around 83% as seen in Table 4. The DBSAFE baseline has an overall accuracy of 84.39%. SVM, Random Forest and CNN perform slightly better even though the difference is negligible. However, KNN performs slightly worse at 82.98%. For this dataset, the performance of the four machine learning algorithms is comparable to DBSAFE.

Table 4. Comparison of 5-fold CV accuracy for SEATS dataset.

Roles/Algorithms	KNN	SVM	RF	CNN	DBSAFE
1	100.0%	100.0%	100.0%	100.0%	100.0%
2	99.46%	99.46%	99.46%	99.46%	99.46%
3	84.81%	75.51%	78.93%	84.81%	83.19%
4	51.98%	37.09%	37.09%	37.09%	37.09%
5	100.0%	100.0%	100.0%	100.0%	100.0%
6	61.82%	97.54%	92.74%	86.19%	86.79%
Total	82.98%	84.90%	84.67%	84.56%	84.39%

1: Find Flights. 2: Find Open Seats. 3: Update Customer. 4: New Reservation.
5: Update Reservation. 6: Delete Reservation.

In general, the misclassification for the SEATS benchmark comes from three of the six roles as seen in Fig. 3. First of all, we have Update Customer which has a significant amount of its queries misclassified to Delete Reservation. All the systems we have tested misclassify queries from New Reservation to either Update Customer, Update Reservation or Delete Reservation.

The misclassification of Update Customer to Delete Reservation might come from the fact that both of those roles do the updateFrequentFlyer query. Vice versa, it could also explain why some queries from Delete Reservation are misclassified to Update Customer.

Misclassification from New Reservation to Update Reservation can be explained by the fact that they share two queries while misclassification from

New Reservation to Delete Reservation is due to the both of them updating customers and frequent flyers information. This is also the case for misclassification to Update Customer.

SmallBank. For SmallBank, the algorithms has an accuracy of around 35% as seen in Table 5. SVM, Random Forest and CNN perform similarly at 39%. However, KNN performs slightly worse at 33.84%. For this dataset, the performance of the four machine learning algorithms is better than DBSAFE at 30.52%.

[DBSAFE]

Roles	1	2	3	4	5	6
1	1666	0	0	0	0	0
2	9	1657	0	0	0	0
3	0	0	1386	0	0	280
4	0	0	255	618	425	368
5	0	0	0	0	1666	0
6	0	0	220	0	0	1446

[KNN]

Roles	1	2	3	4	5	6
1	1666	0	0	0	0	0
2	9	1657	0	0	0	0
3	0	0	1413	117	0	136
4	0	0	287	866	425	88
5	0	0	0	0	1666	0
6	0	0	318	318	0	1030

[SVM]

Roles	1	2	3	4	5	6
1	1666	0	0	0	0	0
2	9	1657	0	0	0	0
3	0	0	1258	0	0	408
4	0	0	216	618	425	407
5	0	0	0	0	1666	0
6	0	0	41	0	0	1625

[RF]

Roles	1	2	3	4	5	6
1	1666	0	0	0	0	0
2	9	1657	0	0	0	0
3	0	0	1315	0	0	351
4	0	0	255	618	425	368
5	0	0	0	0	1666	0
6	0	0	121	0	0	1545

[CNN]

Roles	1	2	3	4	5	6
1	1666	0	0	0	0	0
2	9	1657	0	0	0	0
3	0	0	1413	0	0	253
4	0	0	290	618	425	333
5	0	0	0	0	1666	0
6	0	0	230	0	0	1436

1: Find Flights. 2: Find Open Seats. 3: Update Customer. 4: New Reservation. 5: Update Reservation. 6: Delete Reservation

Fig. 3. SEATS confusion matrices.

Table 5. Comparison of 5-fold CV accuracy for SmallBank dataset.

Roles/Algorithms	KNN	SVM	RF	CNN	DBSAFE
1	28.03%	0.000%	0.000%	7.08%	0.000%
2	26.11%	44.42%	37.70%	58.46%	0.000%
3	69.87%	100.0%	100.0%	100.0%	49.88%
4	35.95%	40.64%	40.64%	32.35%	40.52%
5	20.77%	53.36%	60.32%	39.92%	68.01%
6	22.39%	0.000%	0.000%	0.000%	24.79%
Total	33.84%	39.72%	39.76%	39.62%	30.52%

1: Amalgamate. 2: Balance. 3: Deposit Checking. 4: Send Payment. 5: Transact Savings. 6: Write Check.

[DBSAFE]

Roles	1	2	3	4	5	6
1	0	0	591	274	532	269
2	0	0	560	0	585	521
3	0	0	831	835	0	0
4	0	0	677	675	0	314
5	0	0	533	0	1133	0
6	0	0	426	394	433	413

[KNN]

Roles	1	2	3	4	5	6
1	467	206	111	457	158	267
2	132	435	560	111	112	316
3	0	0	1164	169	0	333
4	283	127	281	599	0	376
5	435	244	533	0	346	108
6	98	349	595	169	82	373

[SVM]

Roles	1	2	3	4	5	6
1	0	359	274	591	442	0
2	0	740	560	0	366	0
3	0	0	1666	0	0	0
4	0	314	675	677	0	0
5	0	244	533	0	889	0
6	0	585	820	0	261	0

[RF]

Roles	1	2	3	4	5	6
1	0	315	274	591	486	0
2	0	628	560	0	478	0
3	0	0	1666	0	0	0
4	0	314	675	677	0	0
5	0	128	533	0	1005	0
6	0	503	820	0	343	0

[CNN]

Roles	1	2	3	4	5	6
1	118	466	274	473	335	0
2	0	974	560	0	132	0
3	0	0	1666	0	0	0
4	138	314	675	539	0	0
5	0	468	533	0	665	0
6	0	748	820	0	98	0

1: Amalgamate. 2: Balance. 3: Deposit Checking. 4: Send Payment. 5: Transact Savings. 6: Write Check.

Fig. 4. SmallBank confusion matrices.

The lower accuracy we get for the Smallbank benchmark in Fig. 4 is to be expected as this benchmark has simple schema and queries. The only role that seems to have a high accuracy across multiple benchmarks is Deposit Checking, but other roles are easily misclassified to Deposit Checking. It can be observed that Amalgamate and Write Check have no query classified to them in certain algorithms. There is no query classified to Amalgamate for SVM, RF and DBSAFE's Naïve Bayes while no query classified to Write Check for SVM, RF and CNN. We also have no query to Balance for DBSAFE's Naïve Bayes.

As shown in Table 6, all of the queries by the Amalgamate role, except for zeroCheckingBalance query, are submitted by users of at least two other roles. Besides, the only difference between zeroCheckingBalance query and updateCheckingBalance query is the value used for the update, which our query representation does not capture.

The seemingly good result we get for the DepositChecking might come from the fact that it is the only role with only two types of queries compared to other roles that do at least three. Hence, the re-sampling gives an overall higher number of occurrence of those queries during training, and making those queries more likely to be attributed to this particular role. The same reasoning can be used to explain the fact that Amalgamate and Write Check have a 0% accuracy as those are roles that do the highest number of query types.

TATP. For TATP, the algorithms have an accuracy of around 85% as seen in Table 7. All four machine learning algorithms perform slightly worse than DBSAFE, although the differences are negligible.

Table 6. SmallBank's query type usage per roles.

Role/Query	q1	q2	q3	q4	q5	q6
Amalgamate	1	1	1	1	1	1
Balance	1	1	1	0	0	0
DepositChecking	1	0	0	0	1	0
SendPayment	1	0	1	0	1	0
TransactSavings	1	1	0	1	0	0
GetAccount	1	1	1	0	1	0

q1: GetAccount. q2: GetSavingsBalance. q3: GetCheckingBalance. q4: UpdateSavingsBalance.
q5: UpdateCheckingBalance. q6: ZeroCheckingBalance.

Table 7. Comparison of 5-fold CV accuracy for TATP dataset.

Roles/Algorithms	KNN	SVM	RF	CNN	DBSAFE
1	100.0%	100.0%	100.0%	100.0%	100.0%
2	90.48%	50.91%	50.91%	70.17%	50.91%
3	70.38%	70.17%	70.17%	60.50%	50.98%
4	100.0%	100.0%	100.0%	100.0%	100.0%
5	100.0%	100.0%	100.0%	100.0%	100.0%
6	100.0%	100.0%	100.0%	100.0%	100.0%
7	39.78%	79.34%	79.34%	70.45%	100.0%
Total	85.77%	85.74%	85.74%	85.84%	85.95%

1: Get User Info. 2: Remove Call Forwarding. 3: User Update. 4: Get Number.
5: Get User Data. 6: Call Forwarding. 7: Location Update

For the TATP benchmark results in Fig. 5, we can see that all the confusion comes from Location Update being misclassified to Remove Call Forwarding or User Update, and vice versa. We can also see that when more queries from Location Update are misclassified to one of those two roles, the number of queries from this particular role that are misclassified to Location Update drop.

The confusion between Location Update and User Update comes from them doing the same getSubscriber query. As for the confusion between Location Update and Call Forwarding, it comes from the fact that both of them update the subscriber table based on the s_id of the subscriber.

TPC-C. For TPC-C, the algorithms have an accuracy of around 90% as seen in Table 8. SVM, Random Forest and CNN perform similarly at 90.22%. However, KNN performs slightly worse at 89.02%. For this dataset, the performance of the four machine learning algorithms slightly worse than DBSAFE at 90.27%, even though the differences are negligible.

[DBSAFE]

Roles	1	2	3	4	5	6	7
1	1428	0	0	0	0	0	0
2	0	727	0	0	0	0	701
3	0	0	728	0	0	0	700
4	0	0	0	1428	0	0	0
5	0	0	0	0	1428	0	0
6	0	0	0	0	0	1428	0
7	0	0	0	0	0	0	1428

[KNN] [SVM]

Roles	1	2	3	4	5	6	7
1	1428	0	0	0	0	0	0
2	0	1292	0	0	0	0	136
3	0	0	1005	0	0	0	423
4	0	0	0	1428	0	0	0
5	0	0	0	0	1428	0	0
6	0	0	0	0	0	1428	0
7	0	580	280	0	0	0	568

Roles	1	2	3	4	5	6	7
1	1428	0	0	0	0	0	0
2	0	727	0	0	0	0	701
3	0	0	1002	0	0	0	426
4	0	0	0	1428	0	0	0
5	0	0	0	0	1428	0	0
6	0	0	0	0	0	1428	0
7	0	0	295	0	0	0	1133

[RF] [CNN]

Roles	1	2	3	4	5	6	7
1	1428	0	0	0	0	0	0
2	0	727	0	0	0	0	701
3	0	0	1002	0	0	0	426
4	0	0	0	1428	0	0	0
5	0	0	0	0	1428	0	0
6	0	0	0	0	0	1428	0
7	0	0	295	0	0	0	1133

Roles	1	2	3	4	5	6	7
1	1428	0	0	0	0	0	0
2	0	1002	0	0	0	0	426
3	0	0	864	0	0	0	564
4	0	0	0	1428	0	0	0
5	0	0	0	0	1428	0	0
6	0	0	0	0	0	1428	0
7	0	284	138	0	0	0	1006

1: Get User Info. 2: Remove Call Forwarding. 3: User Update. 4: Get Number.
5: Get User Data. 6: Call Forwarding. 7: Location Update.

Fig. 5. TATP confusion matrices.

The same macro and micro-analysis as the ones made for CH-benCHmark can be made for TPC-C as seen in Fig. 6 with the confusion mainly coming from the three same roles like the ones from CH-benCHmark.

Table 8. Comparison of 5-fold CV accuracy for TPC-C dataset.

Roles/Algorithms	KNN	SVM	RF	CNN	DBSAFE
1	79.60%	73.50%	73.50%	76.25%	85.10%
2	95.05%	95.05%	95.05%	95.05%	95.05%
3	87.15%	100.0%	100.0%	100.0%	100.0%
4	100.0%	100.0%	100.0%	100.0%	100.0%
5	83.30%	82.55%	82.55%	79.95%	71.20%
Total	89.02%	90.22%	90.22%	90.21%	90.27%

1: Payment. 2: New Order. 3: Order Status. 4: Stock Level. 5: Delivery.

[DBSAFE]

Roles	1	2	3	4	5
1	1702	0	298	0	0
2	36	1901	0	63	0
3	0	0	2000	0	0
4	0	0	0	2000	0
5	294	0	282	0	1424

[KNN]

Roles	1	2	3	4	5
1	1592	0	181	0	227
2	36	1901	0	63	0
3	257	0	1743	0	0
4	0	0	0	2000	0
5	52	0	282	0	1666

[SVM]

Roles	1	2	3	4	5
1	1470	0	298	0	232
2	36	1901	0	63	0
3	0	0	2000	0	0
4	0	0	0	2000	0
5	67	0	282	0	1651

[RF]

Roles	1	2	3	4	5
1	1470	0	298	0	232
2	36	1901	0	63	0
3	0	0	2000	0	0
4	0	0	0	2000	0
5	67	0	282	0	1651

[CNN]

Roles	1	2	3	4	5
1	1525	0	298	0	177
2	36	1901	0	63	0
3	0	0	2000	0	0
4	0	0	0	2000	0
5	123	0	282	0	1595

1: Payment. 2: New Order. 3: Order Status. 4: Stock Level. 5: Delivery.

Fig. 6. TPC-C confusion matrices.

5.5   Experimental Results: Extended CH-benCHmark Dataset

We evaluate the performance of the machine learning algorithms on the extended CH-benCHmark. The accuracy for each of the machine learning algorithm are shown in Table 9.

K-Nearest Neighbours. Figure 7b shows the confusion matrix for extended CH-benCHmark for KNN. KNN achieves 100% accuracy for Management and Logistics while 95.92% for Customer. The remaining achieve accuracy ranging from 80% to 90%. Warehouse's queries are misclassified to Marketing, Customer and Business. Consumer's queries are misclassified to Warehouse and Business's to Marketing.

Support Vector Machine. Figure 7c shows the confusion matrix for extended CH-benCHmark for SVM. SVM achieves 100% accuracy for Management, Logistics and Marketing. Customer achieves 97.36% which is still very high. The remaining achieve an accuracy around 80%. The misclassifications are the same as KNN where two roles have a significant amount of queries misclassified to Marketing.

Random Forest. Figure 7d shows the confusion matrix for the extended CH-benCHmark benchmark for Random Forest. Random Forest achieves 100% accuracy for Management, Logistics and Marketing. Customer role achieves an accuracy of 97.36% while the remaining achieve accuracy around 80%. The misclassifications are the same as KNN and SVM.

Convolutional Neural Network. Figure 7e shows the confusion matrix for extended CH-benCHmark for CNN. CNN achieves 100% accuracy for Management, Logistics and Marketing. Customer role achieves an accuracy of 96.46% while the remaining achieve relatively good accuracy around 70% to 80%. The misclassification of roles are similar to the other machine learning algorithms.

DBSAFE's Naïve Bayes. Figure 7a shows the confusion matrix for extended CH-benCHmark for DBSAFE. Naïve Bayes classifier achieves 100% accuracy for Management and Logistics but Marketing achieves a relatively bad accuracy of 50.48%. The remaining achieve relatively good accuracy of around 65% to 85%.

5.6   Comparative Analysis: Extended CH-benchmark Dataset

It is important to compare the performance of the Machine Learning to understand which algorithms perform better for the extended CH-benCHmark dataset.
From Table 9, it can be observed that the machine learning algorithms generally behave similarly across all the roles except DBSAFE which does not have similar accuracy compared to the rest. Random Forest and SVM have the same accuracy for all roles and they have the highest overall accuracy across the machine learning algorithms. KNN, SVM, Random Forest and CNN have a similar overall accuracy of 91% to 93%. DBSAFE, however, only managed to achieve 79.01% accuracy. For the extended CH-benCHmark, our experiments have shown that the other machine learning algorithms outperform DBSAFE's Naïve Bayes classifier.

Table 9. Comparison of 5-fold CV accuracy for extended CH-benCHmark dataset.

Roles/Algorithms	KNN	SVM	RF	CNN	DBSAFE
1	86.79%	83.13%	83.13%	83.49%	68.01%
2	95.92%	97.36%	97.36%	96.46%	73.17%
3	83.07%	79.05%	79.05%	71.79%	82.59%
4	100.0%	100.0%	100.0%	100.0%	100.0%
5	100.0%	100.0%	100.0%	100.0%	100.0%
6	89.02%	100.0%	100.0%	100.0%	50.48%
Total	92.43%	93.22%	93.22%	91.92%	79.01%

1: Warehouse. 2: Customer. 3: Business. 4: Management. 5: Logistics.
6: Marketing

The first observation with this dataset is the fact that DBSAFE seems to have difficulty classifying the queries when we define meaningful roles as seen in Fig. 7. We can also note that in TPC-C, KNN has the highest number of queries from the combined New Order and Payment roles, which are defined as the Customer role in this benchmark, misclassified as queries from the other TPC-C roles. However, in this benchmark, it still fares better compared to DBSAFE with fewer Customer queries misclassified to Warehouse. We also see that in general Warehouse are misclassified as either Customer, Business or Logistic for DBSAFE, and Customer, Business or Marketing queries for the other algorithms. The other misclassification happens between the Business and Marketing queries.

The misclassification from Warehouse to Business comes from deliv-SumOrderAmountSQL query that accesses the same information as the query 19 "discounted revenue", so their representation is the same. The misclassification between Business and Marketing happens because both roles do queries on the amount of achieved revenue which query the same information. Business role does query 17 "small-quantity-order revenue" and Marketing role does query 22 "global sales opportunity" that query the same columns from the same tables.

5.7   Experimental Results: Query2Vec

We assess the performance of the machine learning algorithms when trained using the input vector from Query2Vec. The dataset that we use is the extended CH-benCHmark dataset. We compare the performance of the four machine learning algorithms without the DBSAFE's Naïve Bayes classifier because DBSAFE requires the input to be a quadruplet for the Naïve Bayes classifier to work. Instead, we use Gaussian Naïve Bayes from scikit-learn as a Naïve Bayes classi-

[DBSAFE]

Roles	1	2	3	4	5	6
1	1133	21	242	0	270	0
2	71	1219	0	0	328	48
3	0	0	1376	0	121	169
4	0	0	0	1666	0	0
5	0	0	0	0	1666	0
6	0	0	594	231	0	841

[KNN]

Roles	1	2	3	4	5	6
1	1446	17	68	0	0	135
2	68	1598	0	0	0	0
3	35	0	1384	0	0	247
4	0	0	0	1666	0	0
5	0	0	0	0	1666	0
6	73	0	110	0	0	1483

[SVM]

Roles	1	2	3	4	5	6
1	1385	39	23	0	0	219
2	44	1622	0	0	0	0
3	0	0	1317	0	0	349
4	0	0	0	1666	0	0
5	0	0	0	0	1666	0
6	0	0	0	0	0	1666

[RF]

Roles	1	2	3	4	5	6
1	1385	39	23	0	0	219
2	44	1622	0	0	0	0
3	0	0	1317	0	0	349
4	0	0	0	1666	0	0
5	0	0	0	0	1666	0
6	0	0	0	0	0	1666

[CNN]

Roles	1	2	3	4	5	6
1	1391	33	23	0	0	219
2	59	1607	0	0	0	0
3	0	0	1196	0	121	349
4	0	0	0	1666	0	0
5	0	0	0	0	1666	0
6	0	0	0	0	0	1666

1: Warehouse. 2: Customer. 3: Business. 4: Management. 5: Logistics. 6: Marketing

Fig. 7. Extended CH-Benchmark confusion matrices.

fier in place of DBSAFE. Gaussian Naïve Bayes is chosen because it is suited to the binary feature which is the input format of our data.

K-Nearest Neighbours. Figure 8b shows the confusion matrix for K-Nearest Neighbours using Query2Vec. The overall accuracy is 99.78%. In KNN, four of the roles achieve 100% accuracy while the other two achieve greater than 99% accuracy. There is a misclassification between Customer and Marketing.

Support Vector Machine. Figure 8c shows the confusion matrix for Support Vector Machine using Query2Vec. The overall accuracy is 78.80%. The results for SVM is not as good as compared to the other algorithms. Two roles has high accuracy of 100% and 98.62% while the rest of the roles achieve accuracy that ranges from 50% to 80%.

Random Forest. Figure 8d shows the confusion matrix for Random Forest using Query2Vec. The overall accuracy is 99.78%. Random Forest performs just slightly worse than KNN. It still achieves very high accuracy with five roles achieving 100% accuracy while the other one achieves around 99%.

Convolutional Neural Network. Figure 8e shows the confusion matrix for Convolutional Neural Network using Query2Vec. The overall accuracy is 98.64%. The algorithm performs just slightly worse than KNN or Random Forest, but it is still much better than SVM. It achieves 100% accuracy in four roles while the remaining achieve accuracy in the range of 93% to 98%.

Gaussian Naïve Bayes. Figure 8a shows the confusion matrix for Gaussian Naïve Bayes using Query2Vec. The overall accuracy is 69.7%. The algorithm performs the worst compared to the rest. Only 1 role achieves 100% accuracy. The worst role achieves 22.78%. The remaining achieve accuracy in the range of 50% to 80%.

5.8   Comparative Analysis: Query2Vec with Extended CH-benCHmark Dataset

From Table 10, it can be observed that KNN, Random Forest and CNN perform very well with Query2Vec vectors with all three algorithms achieving greater than 96% overall accuracy. KNN and Random Forest have near-perfect accuracy. However, SVM and Gaussian Naïve Bayes do not perform as well at 69.66% and 65.72%.

We can see from Fig. 8 that KNN, RF and CNN have the best accuracy with a consistent misclassification of at least eighteen queries between Customer and Warehouse, with CNN misclassifying far more queries between those two roles compared to those two other algorithms. Furthermore, CNN also misclassifies 11 Warehouse queries as Business. On the other hand, SVM and Gaussian Naïve Bayes have less accurate results in general compared to the other three algorithms, with Gaussian Naïve Bayes having the worst accuracy. However, both of

Table 10. Comparison of 5-fold CV accuracy for extended CH-benCHmark dataset using Query2Vec.

Roles/Algorithms	KNN	SVM	RF	CNN	GNB
1	99.16%	98.62%	98.92%	98.56%	70.83%
2	99.76%	100.0%	100.0%	93.52%	50.0%
3	100.0%	50.90%	100.0%	100.0%	22.39%
4	100.0%	100.0%	100.0%	100.0%	100.0%
5	100.0%	78.87%	100.0%	100.0%	78.87%
6	100.0%	79.41%	100.0%	100.0%	96.28%
Total	99.78%	78.80%	99.78%	98.64%	69.7%

1: Warehouse. 2: Customer. 3: Business. 4: Management. 5: Logistics. 6: Marketing

the algorithms still have a 100% accuracy for the queries of the Management role although other queries from other roles are still misclassified to Management.

The remaining misclassification by KNN and RF is happening for the payGet-CustSQL query. This is to be expected as both Warehouse and Customer submit this query. SVM and Gaussian Naïve Bayes poorer results can be attributed to the fact that those two algorithms are not as useful for classification of distance-based vectors compared to the other three algorithms.

[Gaussian Naïve Bayes]

Roles	1	2	3	4	5	6
1	1180	223	240	0	23	0
2	833	833	0	0	0	0
3	170	0	373	0	928	195
4	0	0	0	1666	0	0
5	0	0	0	0	1314	352
6	0	0	0	0	62	1604

[KNN]

Roles	1	2	3	4	5	6
1	1652	14	0	0	0	0
2	4	1662	0	0	0	0
3	0	0	1666	0	0	0
4	0	0	0	1666	0	0
5	0	0	0	0	1666	0
6	0	0	0	0	0	1666

[SVM]

Roles	1	2	3	4	5	6
1	1643	0	0	0	23	0
2	580	1086	0	0	0	0
3	170	0	848	0	580	68
4	0	0	0	1666	0	0
5	0	0	0	0	1314	352
6	0	0	0	63	280	1323

[RF]

Roles	1	2	3	4	5	6
1	1648	18	0	0	0	0
2	0	1666	0	0	0	0
3	0	0	1666	0	0	0
4	0	0	0	1666	0	0
5	0	0	0	0	1666	0
6	0	0	0	0	0	1666

[CNN]

Roles	1	2	3	4	5	6
1	1642	13	11	0	0	0
2	108	1558	0	0	0	0
3	0	0	1666	0	0	0
4	0	0	0	1666	0	0
5	0	0	0	0	1666	0
6	0	0	0	0	0	1666

Roles: 1: Warehouse. 2: Customer. 3: Business. 4: Management. 5: Logistics. 6: Marketing

Fig. 8. Extended CH-Benchmark confusion matrices using Query2Vec.

5.9   Training and Testing Time for Experiments

We measured the training and testing time used for experiments using extended CH-benchmark dataset. CH-benCHmark dataset has 11 tables, 144 columns and it has the largest schema among all the benchmarks. The average time of five folds training on 8,000 samples using KNN, RF, SVM and CNN are 0.421, 0.618, 1.29 and 23.3 s respectively. We observe that CNN requires more time than other machine learning methods and that KNN takes the least training time. In terms of testing time on 2,000 samples, KNN, RF, SVM and CNN take 0.947, 0.0302, 0.436 and 0.214 s respectively. We observe that RF takes the least testing time. For Query2Vec, we also measured the time taken to train all unique queries in extended CH-benchmark dataset. It typically takes about one minute for LSTM autoencoder to train a model that achieves the reconstruction error to be less than 0.01.

5.10   Summary of Experimental Results

We have run experiments comparing the four machine learning algorithms that we have chosen against DBSAFE Naïve Bayes on two datasets: OLTP-Bench benchmark and extended CH-benCHmark. From the OLTP-Bench benchmark, the general trends are that the machine learning algorithms generally perform better than DBSAFE. They outperform DBSAFE in four of the six benchmarks while and they achieve comparable results in the other two. Among the machine learning algorithm themselves, Support Vector Machine, Random Forest and K-Nearest Neighbours generally perform equally well in all the benchmark while KNN performs slightly worse than the other three.

From the results on extended CH-benCHmark using quadruplet, the four machine learning algorithms clearly outperform DBSAFE's accuracy by an average of 12% points.

When we use Query2Vec to create input vectors for the machine learning algorithms, the results vary according to the algorithms. Support Vector Machine with Query2Vec performs much worse with 78.8% compared to using the quadruplet with 93.22%. Both K-Nearest Neighbours and Random Forest achieve 99% accuracy with a 6 to 7% point increase from the model using quadruplet. It should be noted that not all algorithms would fit well to the Query2Vec vectors, as shown from the case of Support Vector Machine.

6   Conclusion

We compared the performance of the DBSAFE's Naïve Bayes classifier with four common machine learning algorithms for classification tasks, namely, K-Nearest Neighbours, Support Vector Machine, Random Forest and Convolutional Neural Network. We used the OLTP-Bench benchmark and a variant of the CH-benCHmark to create synthetic datasets with meaningful hand-crafted roles to comparatively evaluate the performance of the different machine learning algorithms and techniques investigated. The main issue highlighted by these experiment is the need to capture some of the query structure in the feature vector used as input to the machine learning algorithms. We therefore investigated the opportunity to use an embedding technique to represent the structural aspects of the queries into a flat feature vector usable by chosen machine learning algorithms.

Our experiments show that the different machine learning algorithms perform generally better than the original Naïve Bayes classifier. The results also show that a query embedding mechanism such as Query2Vec improves the performance, with two algorithms yielding near-perfect classification.

Generally, we have identified the challenging need for the design of novel embedding mechanisms able to capture the complex structure of queries sufficiently, of query execution plans adorned with optimiser statistics and of transactions with their temporal aspects, in order to prepare adequate feature vectors for input to machine learning classifiers.

Acknowledgement. This research is supported by the National Research Foundation, Prime Minister's Office, Singapore under its Corporate Laboratory@University Scheme, National University of Singapore, and Singapore Telecommunications Ltd.

References

1. Alomari, M., Cahill, M., Fekete, A., Rohm, U.: The cost of serializability on platforms that use snapshot isolation. In: 2008 IEEE 24th International Conference on Data Engineering, pp. 576–585 (2008). https://doi.org/10.1109/ICDE.2008. 4497466
2. Altman, N.S.: An introduction to kernel and nearest-neighbor nonparametric regression. Am. Stat. **46**(3), 175–185 (1992). https://doi.org/10.1080/00031305. 1992.10475879. https://amstat.tandfonline.com/doi/abs/10.1080/00031305.1992. 10475879
3. Angkanawaraphan, V., Pavlo, A.: AuctionMark: A benchmark for high-performance OLTP systems. https://hstore.cs.brown.edu/projects/auctionmark/
4. Baldi, P.: Autoencoders, unsupervised learning, and deep architectures. In: Proceedings of ICML Workshop on Unsupervised and Transfer Learning, pp. 37–49 (2012)
5. Bengio, Y., Courville, A., Vincent, P.: Representation learning: a review and new perspectives. IEEE Trans. Pattern Anal. Mach. Intell. **35**(8), 1798–1828 (2013). https://doi.org/10.1109/TPAMI.2013.50
6. Bengio, Y., Ducharme, R., Vincent, P., Jauvin, C.: A neural probabilistic language model. J. Mach. Learn. Res. **3**, 1137–1155 (2003)
7. Bertino, E., Terzi, E., Kamra, A., Vakali, A.: Intrusion detection in RBAC-administered databases. In: 21st Annual Computer Security Applications Conference (ACSAC 2005), pp. 10–182 (2005). https://doi.org/10.1109/CSAC.2005. 33
8. Boser, B.E., Guyon, I.M., Vapnik, V.N.: A training algorithm for optimal margin classifiers. In: Proceedings of the Fifth Annual Workshop on Computational Learning Theory, COLT 1992, pp. 144–152. ACM, New York (1992). https://doi.org/ 10.1145/130385.130401. http://doi.acm.org.libproxy1.nus.edu.sg/10.1145/130385. 130401

9. Breiman, L.: Random forests. Mach. Learn. **45**(1), 5–32 (2001). https://doi.org/10.1023/A:1010933404324

10. Bu, S.J., Cho, S.B.: A convolutional neural-based learning classifier system for detecting database intrusion via insider attack. Inf. Sci. **512**, 123–136 (2020). https://doi.org/10.1016/j.ins.2019.09.055. http://www.sciencedirect.com/science/article/pii/S0020025519309004

11. Hsu, C.-W., Lin, C.-J.: A comparison of methods for multiclass support vector machines. IEEE Trans. Neural Netw. **13**(2), 415–425 (2002). https://doi.org/10.1109/72.991427

12. Chung, C.Y., Gertz, M., Levitt, K.: DEMIDS: a misuse detection system for database systems. In: van Biene-Hershey, M.E., Strous, L. (eds.) Integrity and Internal Control in Information Systems. ITIFIP, vol. 37, pp. 159–178. Springer, Boston, MA (2000). https://doi.org/10.1007/978-0-387-35501-6_12

13. Cole, R., et al.: The mixed workload CH-benCHmark. In: Proceedings of the Fourth International Workshop on Testing Database Systems, p. 8. ACM (2011)

14. Cortes, C., Vapnik, V.: Support-vector networks. Mach. Learn. **20**(3), 273–297 (1995). https://doi.org/10.1007/BF00994018

15. Cover, T., Hart, P.: Nearest neighbor pattern classification. IEEE Trans. Inf. Theory **13**(1), 21–27 (1967). https://doi.org/10.1109/TIT.1967.1053964

16. Difallah, D.E., Pavlo, A., Curino, C., Cudre-Mauroux, P.: OLTP-bench: an extensible testbed for benchmarking relational databases. Proc. VLDB Endow. **7**(4), 277–288 (2013). https://doi.org/10.14778/2732240.2732246

17. Gongxing, W., Yimin, H.: Design of a new intrusion detection system based on database. In: 2009 International Conference on Signal Processing Systems, pp. 814–817 (2009). https://doi.org/10.1109/ICSPS.2009.139

18. Hastie, T., Friedman, J., Tibshirani, R.: The Elements of Statistical Learning: Data Mining, Inference, and Prediction. Springer Series in Statistics. Springer, New York (2001). https://doi.org/10.1007/978-0-387-21606-5

19. Hinton, G.E., et al.: Learning distributed representations of concepts. In: Proceedings of the Eighth Annual Conference of the Cognitive Science Society, Amherst, MA, vol. 1, p. 12 (1986)

20. Hochreiter, S., Schmidhuber, J.: Long short-term memory. Neural Comput. **9**, 1735–1780 (1997). https://doi.org/10.1162/neco.1997.9.8.1735

21. Hussain, S.R., Sallam, A.M., Bertino, E.: DetAnom: detecting anomalous database transactions by insiders. In: Proceedings of the 5th ACM Conference on Data and Application Security and Privacy, CODASPY 2015, pp. 25–35. ACM, New York (2015). https://doi.org/10.1145/2699026.2699111. http://doi.acm.org/10.1145/2699026.2699111

22. Jain, S., Howe, B., Yan, J., Cruanes, T.: Query2Vec: an evaluation of NLP techniques for generalized workload analytics (2018)

23. Kamra, A., Terzi, E., Bertino, E.: Detecting anomalous access patterns in relational databases. VLDB J. **17**(5), 1063–1077 (2008). https://doi.org/10.1007/s00778-007-0051-4

24. Keller, J.M., Gray, M.R., Givens, J.A.: A fuzzy k-nearest neighbor algorithm. IEEE Trans. Syst. Man Cybern. SMC **15**(4), 580–585 (1985). https://doi.org/10.1109/TSMC.1985.6313426

25. Khraisat, A., Gondal, I., Vamplew, P., Kamruzzaman, J.: Survey of intrusion detection systems: techniques, datasets and challenges. Cybersecurity **2**(1), 20 (2019). https://doi.org/10.1186/s42400-019-0038-7

26. Le, Q., Mikolov, T.: Distributed representations of sentences and documents. In: International Conference on Machine Learning, pp. 1188–1196 (2014)

27. LeCun, Y., et al.: Backpropagation applied to handwritten zip code recognition. Neural Comput. **1**(4), 541–551 (1989). https://doi.org/10.1162/neco.1989.1.4.541

28. LeCun, Y., Bottou, L., Bengio, Y., Haffner, P., et al.: Gradient-based learning applied to document recognition. Proc. IEEE **86**(11), 2278–2324 (1998)

29. Li, J., Luong, M.T., Jurafsky, D.: A hierarchical neural autoencoder for paragraphs and documents. arXiv preprint arXiv:1506.01057 (2015)

30. Liaw, A., Wiener, M.: Classification and regression by randomforest. Forest **2**(3), 18–22 (2001)

31. Lu, S., Wei, X., Li, Y., Wang, L.: Detecting anomaly in big data system logs using convolutional neural network. In: 2018 IEEE 16th Intl Conf on Dependable, Autonomic and Secure Computing, 16th Intl Conf on Pervasive Intelligence and Computing, 4th Intl Conf on Big Data Intelligence and Computing and Cyber Science and Technology Congress (DASC/PiCom/DataCom/CyberSciTech), pp. 151–158. IEEE (2018)

32. Luong, M.T., Pham, H., Manning, C.D.: Effective approaches to attention-based neural machine translation. arXiv preprint arXiv:1508.04025 (2015)

33. Mathew, S., Petropoulos, M., Ngo, H.Q., Upadhyaya, S.: A data-centric approach to insider attack detection in database systems. In: Jha, S., Sommer, R., Kreibich, C. (eds.) RAID 2010. LNCS, vol. 6307, pp. 382–401. Springer, Heidelberg (2010). https://doi.org/10.1007/978-3-642-15512-3_20

34. Mazzawi, H., Dalal, G., Rozenblatz, D., Ein-Dorx, L., Niniox, M., Lavi, O.: Anomaly detection in large databases using behavioral patterning. In: 2017 IEEE 33rd International Conference on Data Engineering (ICDE), pp. 1140–1149 (2017). https://doi.org/10.1109/ICDE.2017.158

35. Mikolov, T., Chen, K., Corrado, G., Dean, J.: Efficient estimation of word representations in vector space. arXiv preprint arXiv:1301.3781 (2013)

36. Mikolov, T., Sutskever, I., Chen, K., Corrado, G.S., Dean, J.: Distributed representations of words and phrases and their compositionality. In: Advances in Neural Information Processing Systems, pp. 3111–3119 (2013)

37. Neuvonen, S., Wolski, A., Manner, M., Raatikka, V.: Telecommunication application transaction processing (TATP) benchmark description 1.0 (2009)

38. Roichman, A., Gudes, E.: DIWeDa - detecting intrusions in web databases. In: Atluri, V. (ed.) DBSec 2008. LNCS, vol. 5094, pp. 313–329. Springer, Heidelberg (2008). https://doi.org/10.1007/978-3-540-70567-3_24

39. Ronao, C.A., Cho, S.B.: Anomalous query access detection in RBAC-administered databases with random forest and PCA. Inf. Sci. **369**, 238–250 (2016). https://doi.org/10.1016/j.ins.2016.06.038

40. Rutkowski, L., Jaworski, M., Pietruczuk, L., Duda, P.: Decision trees for mining data streams based on the Gaussian approximation. IEEE Trans. Knowl. Data Eng. **26**(1), 108–119 (2014)

41. Sallam, A., Bertino, E.: Detection of temporal data ex-filtration threats to relational databases. In: 2018 IEEE 4th International Conference on Collaboration and Internet Computing (CIC), pp. 146–155 (2018). https://doi.org/10.1109/CIC.2018.00030

42. Sallam, A., Bertino, E.: Result-based detection of insider threats to relational databases. In: Ahn, G., Thuraisingham, B.M., Kantarcioglu, M., Krishnan, R. (eds.) Proceedings of the Ninth ACM Conference on Data and Application Security and Privacy, CODASPY 2019, Richardson, TX, USA, 25–27 March 2019, pp. 133–143. ACM (2019). https://doi.org/10.1145/3292006.3300039

43. Sallam, A., Bertino, E.: Techniques and systems for anomaly detection in database systems. In: Calo, S., Bertino, E., Verma, D. (eds.) Policy-Based Autonomic Data Governance. LNCS, vol. 11550, pp. 113–133. Springer, Cham (2019). https://doi.org/10.1007/978-3-030-17277-0_7

44. Sallam, A., Bertino, E., Hussain, S.R., Landers, D., Lefler, R.M., Steiner, D.: DBSAFE - an anomaly detection system to protect databases from exfiltration attempts. IEEE Syst. J. **11**(2), 483–493 (2017). https://doi.org/10.1109/JSYST.2015.2487221

45. Sallam, A., Fadolalkarim, D., Bertino, E., Xiao, Q.: Data and syntax centric anomaly detection for relational databases. Wiley Interdiscip. Rev. Data Min. Knowl. Discov. **6**(6), 231–239 (2016). https://doi.org/10.1002/widm.1195

46. Sallam, A., Xiao, Q., Bertino, E., Fadolalkarim, D.: Anomaly detection techniques for database protection against insider threats (invited paper). In: 2016 IEEE 17th International Conference on Information Reuse and Integration (IRI), pp. 20–29 (2016). https://doi.org/10.1109/IRI.2016.12

47. Sandhu, R.S., Coyne, E.J., Feinstein, H.L., Youman, C.E.: Role-based access control models. Computer **29**(2), 38–47 (1996). https://doi.org/10.1109/2.485845

48. Schmidhuber, J.: Deep learning in neural networks: an overview. Neural Netw. **61**, 85–117 (2015). https://doi.org/10.1016/j.neunet.2014.09.003

49. Shebaro, B., Sallam, A., Kamra, A., Bertino, E.: PostgreSQL anomalous query detector. In: Joint 2013 EDBT/ICDT Conferences, EDBT 2013 Proceedings, Genoa, Italy, 18–22 March 2013, pp. 741–744 (2013). https://doi.org/10.1145/2452376.2452469

50. Singh, I., Sareen, S., Ahuja, H.: Detection of malicious transactions in databases using dynamic sensitivity and weighted rule mining. In: 2017 International Conference on Innovations in Information, Embedded and Communication Systems (ICIIECS), pp. 1–8 (2017). https://doi.org/10.1109/ICIIECS.2017.8276084

51. Singh, M.P., Sural, S., Vaidya, J., Atluri, V.: Managing attribute-based access control policies in a unified framework using data warehousing and in-memory database. Comput. Secur. **86**, 183–205 (2019). https://doi.org/10.1016/j.cose.2019.06.001. http://www.sciencedirect.com/science/article/pii/S0167404819301166

52. Smola, A.J., et al.: Regression estimation with support vector learning machines. Ph.D. thesis, Master's thesis, Technische Universität München (1996)

53. Stonebraker, M., Pavlo, A.: The seats airline ticketing systems benchmark. http://hstore.cs.brown.edu/projects/seats

54. Ho, T.K.: Random decision forests. In: Proceedings of 3rd International Conference on Document Analysis and Recognition, vol. 1, pp. 278–282 (1995). https://doi.org/10.1109/ICDAR.1995.598994

55. Transaction Processing Performance Council (TPC): TPC Benchmark C Standard Specification (2010). Revision 5.11

56. Transaction Processing Performance Council (TPC): TPC Benchmark E, Standard Specification. Version 1.14.0 (2015). http://www.tpc.org/tpce/

57. Transaction Processing Performance Council (TPC): TPC Benchmark H Standard Specification (2018). Revision 2.18.0

58. Vapnik, V.: Pattern recognition using generalized portrait method. Autom. Remote Control **24**, 774–780 (1963)

Top-k Queries over Distributed Uncertain Categorical Data

Adel Benaissa, Soror Sahri$^{(\boxtimes)}$, and Mourad Ouziri

Université de Paris, Paris, France
benaissa.adel@gmail.com, {soror.sahri,mourad.ouziri}@parisdescartes.fr

Abstract. Uncertain data arises in many modern applications including sensor networks, data integration, and information extraction. Often this data is distributed and there is a need to do efficient query processing over the data in situ. We focus on answering top-k queries and propose a distributed algorithm TDUD, to efficiently answer top-k queries over distributed uncertain categorical data in queries single round of communication. TDUD uses a distributed index structure composed of local uncertain indexes (LUIs) on local sites and a single global uncertain index (GUI) on a coordinator site. Our algorithm minimizes the amount of communication needed to answer a top-k query by maintaining the mean sum dispersion of the probability distribution on each site. Extensive experiments are conducted to verify the effectiveness and efficiency of the proposed methods in terms of communication costs and response time. We show empirically that TDUD is near-optimal in that it can typically retrieve the top-k query answers by communicating only k tuples in a single round.

Keywords: Distributed databases · Distributed indexing · Uncertain data · Top-k query

1 Introduction

Recently, there has been much interest in uncertain data management in many application areas such as data integration, data cleaning, information extraction, etc. [3,5,10,18]. Data may be uncertain due to differences in sensor readings, delays in data transfer, or differences in data entry. Existing work in this area provides new models for uncertain data, prototype implementations, and efficient query processing algorithms. Most of this work uses a possible world semantics, where each possible world corresponds to a single deterministic data instance [10]. Many applications where uncertainty arises are distributed in nature, e.g., distributed sensor networks or the integration of multiple distributed data sources [11,15,17,21]. However, existing techniques including solutions for indexing and query processing over uncertain data were mainly proposed in centralized environments [3,9,10,18], and do not account for distribution. As a result, it is still a challenging issue to efficiently process queries over distributed

© Springer-Verlag GmbH Germany, part of Springer Nature 2020
A. Hameurlain and A Min Tjoa (Eds.): TLDKS XLIII, LNCS 12130, pp. 40–61, 2020.
https://doi.org/10.1007/978-3-662-62199-8_2

uncertain data. Notable exceptions include recent work on indexing [6,17] and query processing of distributed uncertain data [2,4,11,15,17,21,22]. This work has only considered top-k queries over uncertain real-valued attributes. Furthermore, in many domains, data records are composed of a set of descriptive attributes, many of which are neither numeric nor inherently ordered in any way. Values without an inherent distance measure defined over them are called *categorical* [18]. In this paper, we address the problem of distributed top-k query processing over uncertain categorical data represented as a set of values with associated probabilities. We propose an approach that efficiently answers queries over distributed uncertain data with minimum communication and processing costs, using a distributed index structure.

T_{id}	Weight	Illness
t_1	700	$\{(mc, 0.1); fa(0.9)\}$
t_2	710	$\{(mc, 0.75); fa(0.25)\}$
t_3	790	$\{(mc, 1)\}$
t_4	725	$\{(mc, 0.55); (fa, 0.45)\}$

(a) Relation R_1

T_{id}	Weight	Illness
t_5	700	$\{(mc, 0.6); fa(0.4)\}$
t_6	710	$\{(mc, 0.92); fa(0.08)\}$
t_7	790	$\{(mc, 0.85); (fa, 0.15)\}$
t_8	725	$\{(mc, 0.95); (fa, 0.05)\}$

(b) Relation R_2

T_{id}	Weight	Illness
t_9	749	$\{(mc, 0.65); nc(0.35)\}$
t_{10}	645	$\{(mc, 0.45); nc(0.55)\}$
t_{11}	801	$\{(mc, 0.9); nc(0.1)\}$
t_{12}	799	$\{(mc, 0.55); (nc, 0.45)\}$

(c) Relation R_3

T_{id}	Weight	Illness
t_{13}	711	$\{(mc, 0.65); fa(0.35)\}$
t_{14}	745	$\{(fa, 0.2); (mc, 0.8)\}$
t_{15}	901	$\{(nc, 0.55); (mc, 0.45)\}$
t_{16}	799	$\{(nc, 0.8); (mc, 0.2)\}$

(d) Relation R_4

Fig. 1. Example of distributed uncertain relation R

Example 1. Let's motivate the approach through an example. Consider the relation $Farm$ that stores bovine records on multiple nodes including different breeders and veterinarians and is specified by the schema: $Farm(T_{id}, weight, illness)$ where the *illness* attribute specifies the illnesses that can affect a cow. *Illness* is an uncertain attribute that takes values from the categorical domain $\{mc, fa, ns, ...\}$, where: (mc) means *mad cow*, (fa) means *fever accurate* and (nc) means *normal cow*, etc. Let R be a relation instance of $Farm$. In Fig. 1, the relations R_1, R_2, R_3 and R_4 are distributed horizontal partitions of R. The first tuple in R_1 specifies that the cow with the identifier t_1, has a weight of 700 and its illness may be *(mc)* with the probability 0.1 and may be *accurate fever (fa)* with the probability 0.9.

An interesting query for breeders and insurers is the following:

Q_1 : *Find the four cows that are most likely affected by mad cow (mc) disease.*

This is a top-k query over uncertain data. A straightforward and naive approach to answer such a query is to ask all distributed nodes to send their top-k

tuples to a coordinating node[1]. The coordinating node can then combine the results to return the actual top-k. However, this approach requires all nodes to send k tuples in a single round of communication. Benaissa et al. [6,7] proposed a better algorithm for distributed top-k query processing that uses two rounds of communication but requires significantly fewer tuples to be exchanged[2]. Their approach maintains a global index (GUI) that holds for each possible value, the highest probability of that value located at each node. In the first round, the algorithm requests the kth highest probability from all nodes. Using this information and the GUI, in the second round, a smaller set of tuples are retrieved (typically much smaller than the number of nodes times of k) that are still guaranteed to contain the top-k. We illustrate the approach using the example.

Example 2. Returning to Example 1, for the value mc, the GUI would contain the highest probabilities for each node, that is, $max(R_1) = 1, max(R_2) = 0.95, max(R_3) = 0.9$ and $max(R_4) = 0.8$. To answer a top-4 query, in the first round, the coordinator asks all nodes to send the fourth highest probability (in this example, this would be $R_1(0.1)$, $R_2(0.6)$, $R_3(0.45)$, $R_4(0.2)$). The coordinator chooses the highest value (0.6) to be a conservative lower-bound estimate for the k_{th} value (called τ). In the second communication round, any node whose max value is less than τ is pruned (in this example, no nodes are pruned). For all remaining nodes, we request all tuples with probability greater than or equal to τ. In this example, R_1 would send 2 tuples, R_2 would send 4, R_3 2, and R_4 only 1 as depicted in Fig. 2(a), so the total cost of this round is 9 (tuples). Finally, the query coordinator picks the top-4 from the candidate tuples (t_2 from R_1, t_8 and t_6 from R_2 and t_{11} from R_3), as depicted in Fig. 2.b. The total communication cost of the approach is 13 tuples (four, or k from Round 1, and 9 from Round 2). Notice that this approach is a conservative one that reduces the communication cost (from 16 to 9 tuples in this example) and is guaranteed to produce the correctness result.

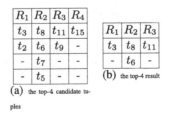

Fig. 2. Result of the second round

An important drawback of DUTk is that it requires two rounds of communication rather than one for NAIV. In distributed environments each round of communication must wait for the last node to respond, so slow nodes (*stragglers*)

---

[1] We will call this approach NAIV in our experiments.
[2] We will call this approach DUTk in our experiments.

can significantly reduce performance for multiple-round algorithms. In addition, DUTk is conservative and may require the retrieval of many more than k tuples (tuples that do not contribute to the answer), especially for high values of k. In order to address these drawbacks, we propose an algorithm that uses a single round of communication and a much more aggressive pruning strategy that is often able to avoid contacting nodes that do not contain a query answer. Hence, the single round of communication is often among a much smaller set of nodes, greatly improving response times. The idea is to enrich the GUI with one additional, well-chosen, summary statistic that can be used to determine if nodes are unlikely to have top-k tuples. The summary statistic is computed over a distribution and reflects how dense the top of the distribution at a node is. In the example the distribution for R_1, R_2, R_3 is bunched at the top, while R_4 is not and our summary statistic will reflect this. Knowing this, we could, for example, ask R_2 for 2 values, R_1 for 1 value.

In summary, our contributions are as follows.

- We propose a top level global uncertain index (GUI) on a coordinator node. The global index extends the GUI of Benaissa et al. [6,7] to include a novel summary statistic, the *mean sum dispersion* of the probability distribution on each node.
- A distributed algorithm, referred as TDUD, to efficiently process top-k queries over distributed and uncertain categorical data. The algorithm performs a *distributed k-bound pruning*, where the distributed sites whose tuples are not likely to be a part of the query answer, are pruned thanks to the Global index. Then it computes the threshold probability to prune tuples from selected local nodes accordingly. Finally, selected tuples are ranked on the coordinator node. We show the GUI can be used to provide high quality answers while reducing the communication cost, local node load, and query response time.
- We conducted experimental studies to show that TDUD significantly reduces the number of tuples exchanged (over NAIV, DUTk, and variants of TDUD that use different summary statistics). We also show that TDUD improves response time over NAIV by requiring the single communication round to use many fewer nodes.

The rest of the paper is organized as follows. Section 2 presents the uncertain model and the top-k query semantics that we use. In Sect. 3, we present our distributed indexing technique and we describe the top-k query processing using the distributed index in Sect. 4. In Sect. 5, we present an experimental evaluation of our proposed framework. Related work is presented in Sect. 6, and finally we conclude the paper in Sect. 7.

2 Problem Definition

In this section, we present our data model, and discuss the semantics of top-k queries over distributed and uncertain categorical data. We finally present our proposed framework.

2.1 Uncertain Data Model

Uncertainty can be identified both at the tuple level [8], as well as at the attribute level. In this paper, we consider the attribute-level uncertainty model [5]. While, the value of uncertain attributed is relevant from categorical data. The uncertain data in our work are modelled as a probabilistic database horizontally distributed over a set of sites $\mathcal{S} = \{S_1, S_2, ..., S_m\}$ such that $\mathcal{S} = \underset{i \in [1,m]}{\cup} S_i$ and $S_i \cap S_j = \emptyset$, for $i, j \in [1, m], i \neq j$.

In the rest of the paper, we refer to the database name as its site name. Each local database S_i has n_i tuples with uncertain attribute values. We note that our approach also works for several attributes. For the sake of simplicity and without loss of generality, we limit the discussion to relations with a single uncertain attribute from a categorical domain [18].

Let $\mathcal{S}.A$ be a particular attribute in $\mathcal{S}$ which is uncertain. The attribute $\mathcal{S}.A$ takes values from a categorical domain D with cardinality $|D| = N$. For a traditional (certain) relation, the value of an attribute A for each tuple $t.A$ would be a single value in D. For an uncertain relation, the value of a tuple $t.a$ is a probability distribution over D. Let $D = \{d_1, d_2, ..., d_N\}$, then each value of $t.A$ from D has probability $P(t.A = d_l)$ for $l \in 1, ..., N$ such that $\sum_{l=1}^{N} P(t.A = d_l) = 1$.

2.2 Distributed Uncertain Top-k Queries

There has been much interest in answering top-k queries on uncertain data, known as ranking query answers on probabilistic data in a centralized way. The ranking functions have treated the top-k problem using different semantics. The most important of them are U-top-k [19], U-krank [20], and Pt-topk [12]. The U-Top-k returns k tuples with the highest probability of being in the top-k result across all possible worlds. U-krank returns a set of k tuples where the ith is the most probable tuple to appear in the ith rank across all possible worlds. Finally, Pt-topk is a probability-based threshold query that returns all tuples whose probability of being in the top-k is above a given threshold.

In the majority of the works tackled, the top-k queries are based on combining the score and likelihood to provide different results. In our work, we consider top-k selection queries over distributed and uncertain categorical data as problem we call TDUD that has the following definition.

Definition 21 *(Top-k Query Answer)*
Given a distributed uncertain relation $\mathcal{S} = \underset{i \in [1,m]}{\cup} R_i$ *and selection query* $\sigma_{A=d}(\mathcal{S})$ *over the uncertain attribute* A, *the top-k query answer is the set of (at least) k tuples with the k highest probabilities among all tuples in* $\{t \in \mathcal{S} | t.A = d\}$.

2.3 General Framework

The inputs of our query processing approach are: an uncertain database over distributed sites $\mathcal{S} = \{S_1, S_2, ..., S_m\}$ and a distributed uncertain top-k query

Q. The aim of our approach is to efficiently answer top-k queries over uncertain distributed data with minimal communication and processing costs. This is performed in two main phases. We describe them in the following sections:

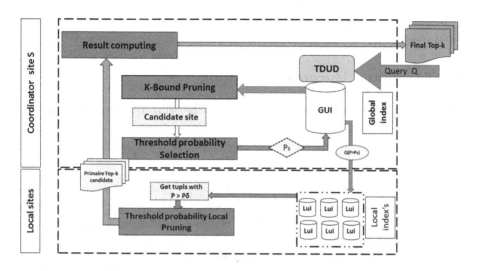

Fig. 3. An overview of the general framework

We enhance the distributed indexing technique (global uncertain index or GUI) of Benaissa et al. [6]. We maintain the same local index LUI proposed by of Benaissa et al. [6,7]. In our work, the distributed indexing techniques are based on a two-level hierarchical index:

- **Local uncertain index (LUI)**: We maintain the same index structure proposed by Shin et al. [18]. This indexing consists of building a local index at each local site.
- **Global uncertain index (GUI)**: We enhance the distributed indexing technique (global uncertain index or GUI) of Benaissa et al. [6,7]. In particular, we enrich the global index structure with more relevant information that summarizes the local indexes.

By leveraging the indexing technique, the framework integrates a distributed algorithm TDUD to process top-k queries in one round of communication. The main steps of this algorithm (depicted in Fig. 3) are the following.

- Distributed k-bound pruning. This step, performed on the global uncertain index or GUI, by using the more relevant information that summarizes the local indexes. It allows the computation of an approximate k-bound probability (τ) such that all top-k query answers are likely to have a probability less than this bound.

- Threshold probability pruning. This step uses τ at each site tuples to locally prune that are not involved in the final result of the top-k query.
- Result ranking. This step merges the query results of local sites and ranks them to return the final top-k query result.

In what follows, we present the index structures and details of the main steps of our algorithm.

3　Distributed Uncertain Indexing

In this section, we present the main process for building local and global uncertain indexes.

3.1　Local Uncertain Index Structure

For indexing uncertain data on each local site, we adopted the inverted index based structure proposed by Singh et al. [18]. That is, for each value $d \in D$ of an uncertain attribute A, we store in an inverted index sets of pairs including the tuple id and probability for every tuple with value d. This list is organized in decreasing order of probability. In practice, such a list may be organized in memory with a dynamic structure like a B+Tree. The main advantage of local indexing is that it can be leveraged easily for top-k selection queries. Figure 4 depicts the local index of relation R_1 of site S_1 from Example 1.

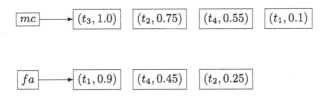

Fig. 4. Local uncertain index (LUI) on site S_1

3.2　Global Uncertain Index Structure

In this section, we describe the structure of the global uncertain index. It determines which local indexes should be accessed for a given query. Hence, the GUI should be stored on the query site, which we referred to as the coordinator. In this work, we enrich the GUI proposed by Benaissa et al. [6,7], with more summarizing information from the local indexes LUIs. This additional information allows an early pruning (at the coordinator) of an important number of sites whose tuples do not belong to the query result. The pruning of sites limits the rounds of communication between the coordinator and the distributed sites to only one round which in turn reduces the communication cost. This improves the efficiency of the query evaluation approach.

Given a distributed relation S, the GUI is an inverted index based structure on the uncertain attribute A of S. It summarizes information of the local indexes LUIs. As for the local indexes, entries in a GUI correspond to the categorical domain values of A. For each entry $d \in D$ and for each site S that contains a tuple with value d, the GUI contains a triple (S, P_{max}, M). The value P_{max} is the maximum probability of any tuple in S with value d ($S.A = d$). The value M is a *local summarizing measure* (defined in the next section) that captures the distribution of the probabilities of all tuples on the site where $S.A = d$.

Local Summarizing Measure. For the sake of simplicity and without loss of generality, let us consider $V = \{P_1, P_2, ..., P_n\}$ a vector of probabilities ($n \geq 1$) on a site S for a value d that is stored in the LUI of S in descending order. Hence, $P_{max} = P_1$. We could summarize this probability distribution using familiar metrics for summarizing data (e.g., the *mean, standard deviation, mean absolute deviation*). However, these measures are not tailored for answering top-k queries.

We propose a summarizing measure that leverages the mean of the sum of dispersion between the maximal value of V and each element of this vector. Our goal is to have a (small) summary that gives a good indication of how dense the top part of the distribution is in order to best estimate the likelihood of a distribution containing top-k query answers. We refer to this measure as *Statistical Dispersion Measure*.

Definition 31. *Statistical Dispersion Measure (SDM) Given a local index LUI on site S and an entry $d \in D$ and its attached probability vector V containing $n \geq 1$ values the statistical dispersion measure $M(S, d)^3$ is:*

$$
M(S, d) = \begin{cases} \dfrac{1}{n-1} \sum_{j=2}^{n} \dfrac{P_{max} - P_j}{j-1} & \text{if } n > 1 \\[2ex] 0 & \text{if } n = 1 \end{cases}
\tag{1}
$$

Based on this summarizing metric, we are able to predict the approximate number of tuples to obtain from each local site and then prune sites that are unlikely to answer top-k query. In the next section, we detail this pruning process. We must remember that the statistical dispersion measure is calculated in offline phase for each $d \in D$ on each site. Consequently, to complete the list of triples for each entry d in the GUI, all LUIs are explored to get the corresponding list of pairs (tuple and probability) for d. Once the list is complete, the triples for an entry d are ordered in decreasing order of their maximum probabilities.

Notice that the index construction is performed offline. The main steps involved in building a GUI are displayed in Algorithm 1.

---

[3] To avoid having a null value of the SDM ($M(S, d)=0$), V should have at least two different values of the attached probabilities. We note that in practice probability values are different.

input : Domain of values D; Distributed relation $\mathcal{S}$
output: **GUI**

for *each $S \in \mathcal{S}$* **do**
   | Build GUI triples from *LUI* of S
   | **for** *each $d \in LUI$* **do**
   | | $M \leftarrow M(S, d)$ computed using Formula (1) of Def 31
   | | $P_{max} \leftarrow$ maximal probability of d in LUI
   | | $Ld \leftarrow (S, P_{max}, M)$
   | **end**
end

for *each $d \in D$* **do**
   | Organize Ld as inverted list in decreasing order of the P_{max} of each S
end
return(**GUI**)

Algorithm 1: Global Uncertain Index (GUI) Construction

Example 3. Let us consider the example of the LUI of S_1 as depicted in Fig. 4. For each entry (*mc* and *fa*) of this LUI, the GUI stores one triple. The triple associated with the value *mc* is $(S_1, 1, 0.065)$ where the value 1 is the maximum probability of the set of pairs associated with *mc* in the LUI of S_1 and the value 0.065 is the summarizing measure that captures the distribution of probabilities associated with *mc* at S_1. In the same way, the triple $(S_1, 0.90, 0.389)$ is associated with the entry *fa*. Figure 5 depicts the GUI for the data of Example 1.

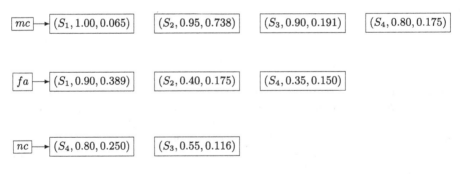

Fig. 5. Global Uncertain Index (GUI)

4 Distributed Top-*k* Processing

Now we come to the most crucial part of this paper: our proposed algorithm. Referred to as TDUD, the algorithm process a distributed uncertain top-k query Q issued from a coordinating site S_c containing a global index GUI assuming data are stored in a set of local sites, each containing an LUI. Assuming that Q is the selection query $\sigma_{A=d}(\mathcal{S})$ from the GUI we retrieve a set of sites containing tuples with value d: $L_Q = \{S_1, S_2, ..., S_h\}$ where $|L_Q| = h \leq m$. Recall that these sites are ordered by their maximum probabilities in the GUI. The TDUD algorithm uses the local summarizing information to prune a maximal number of sites that are unlikely to contain any top-k answers. The idea is to prune all sites with maximal probabilities from L_Q that do not lie within a cutoff threshold τ and then select candidate sites from L_Q with maximal probabilities higher than τ.

---

input : Distributed uncertain relation $\mathcal{S}$; Query $Q = \sigma_{A=d}(\mathcal{S})$; k
output: L_Q list of relevant sites for Q, k

// 1. Pruning sites based on categorical value selection $L_Q \leftarrow GUI(d)$ // 2. Calculate the k-bound pruning
$K' \leftarrow$ k-bound from Equation 4
Discard all sites in L_Q with index $> K'$
// 3. Fix a threshold probability τ
$\tau = P_{max}(S_{K'+1})$
//4. Query processing
Broadcast query to all sites in L_Q: get tuples where $P > \tau$

// final Result computing
$ResultQ \leftarrow$ Rank the result on S_c and select the top-k return($ResultQ$)

Algorithm 2: TDUD: distributed uncertain top-k processing algorithm

---

Consequently, our TDUD algorithm returns a set of tuples from each site $S_i \in L_Q$, such that $P_{max}(S_i) > \tau$ where τ is the estimated cut-off threshold. Before presenting how to estimate the threshold probability τ we present how the k-bound pruning is performed.

4.1   Distributed K-bound Pruning

Our first goal is to estimate (using only the GUI) the number of tuples returned by each site in L_Q (in order). To do this, we estimate the number of tuples in S_1 with probability between $P_{max}(S_2)$ and $P_{max}(S_1)$. If this number is less than k, we continue and estimate the number of tuples on S_1 with probability between $P_{max}(S_3)$ and $P_{max}(S_2)$ and also the number of tuples on S_2 in this same range. We now generalize this to estimate the number of tuples in each of the rectangular regions of Fig. 6.

Given the list L_Q, we wish to estimate the number of tuples in S_i with probabilities between $P_{max}(S_{j+1})$ and the higher value $P_{max}(S_j)$, i.e. between two maximum probabilities of two consecutive sites S_j and S_{j+1}. Here, $i \leq j$.

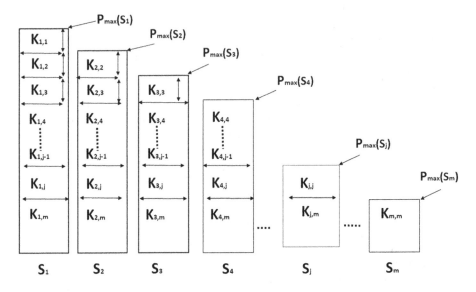

Fig. 6. k-bound rectangles $K(i, j)$

We call this estimate the k-bound $K(i, j)$ and it is computed by the Eq. (2).

$$K(i,j) = \begin{cases} \left\lfloor \dfrac{P_{max}(S_j) - P_{max}(S_{j+1})}{M(S_i, d)} \right\rfloor & \text{if } j < m \\[2em] \left\lfloor \dfrac{P_{max}(S_j)}{M(S_i, d)} \right\rfloor & \text{if } j = m \end{cases} \qquad (2)$$

Each $K(i, j)$ approximates the number of tuples in site S_i having probability between $P_{max}(S_{j+1})$ and $P_{max}(S_j)$]. As depicted in Fig. 7, we need to sum up these estimates to obtain an estimate of both how many sites are likely to contain a top-k answer and also to bound the number of tuples we need to retrieve from each site that may have an answer. To see this, consider $K(1, 1)$. If $K(1, 1) \geq k$ then we only need to request tuples from site S_1 and we only need to request tuples having probability less than $P_{max}(S_2)$.[4] But if $K(1, 1) < k$, then we can consider whether all the top-k tuples are likely to be on sites S_1 and S_2. To do this, we add $K(1, 1)$, $K(1, 2)$ and $K(2, 2)$. This is an estimate of the number of tuples with probabilities less than $P_{max}(S_3)$ on sites S_1 and S_2. Let us call this sum K_2. If $K_2 \geq k$, then TDUD will request tuples from sites S_1 and S_2 having probability less than $P_{max}(S_3)$ as this set is estimated to contain at least k tuples. We now generalize this process.

$$K_l = \sum_{i=1}^{l} \sum_{j=1}^{i} K(i, j) \qquad (3)$$

---

[4] Actually in this case, we can request the top-k tuples approximately.

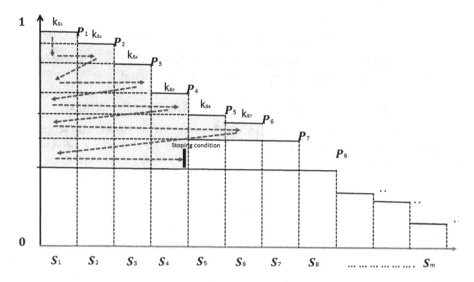

Fig. 7. Cumulative k-bounds K_l

$$K' = \underset{x}{\mathrm{Argmin}}(K_x \geq k) \tag{4}$$

Hence, K' is the lowest l such that $K_l \geq k$.

Example 4. Let us consider the query from Example 1.

Q_1: *Find the four cows most likely to be affected by mc disease* .

The list of sites is $L = \{S_1, S_2, S_3, S_4\}$ which is organized according to the sites maximal probabilities in decreasing order by the inverted list for value mc in the GUI. The k-bounding process will have j iterations where $j <= 4$. At the first iteration ($j = 1$), the k-bound pruning is performed on S_1.

Here, $K(1,1)$ is computed to estimate the number of tuples within the range $[P_{max}(S_1), P_{max}(S_2)]$, i.e. between the two maximal probabilities of the two first sites S_1 and S_2. This is depicted as $K(1,2)$ in Fig. 8.

$$K(1,1) = \frac{P_{max}(S_2) - P_{max}(S_1)}{M(S_1, mc)} \approx 0.77$$

The stopping condition is not satisfied[5], i.e. $K(1,1) < 4$. Hence, we continue with a second iteration. At this iteration, sites S_1 and S_2 are considered. Thus, k-bound is the cumulative sum of the highest probability tuples from S_1 computed at the previous iteration 1 and estimate $K(1,2)$ (an estimate of tuples at S_1 with probabilities between the max on site 2 and the max on site 1), and $K(2,2)$ (an estimate of tuples at S_2 in the same range).

---

[5] In the example, we are reporting the real number estimates but our algorithm takes the integer floor of this number. See Eq. 2.

$$K_2 = K(1,1) + K(1,2) + K(2,2) \approx 1.73$$

The stopping condition is not satisfied, so the k-bound process is continued for $j = 3$. At this iteration, sites S_1, S_2 and S_3 are considered.

$$K_3 = K(1,1) + K(1,2) + K(2,2) + K(1,3) + K(2,3) + K(3,3)$$

In this example, K_3 add up to 4.18 which rounds to 4. Hence, the stopping condition is satisfied and we have K' = 3. As a result, site 4 does not need to be visited to retrieve the top-4 answers.

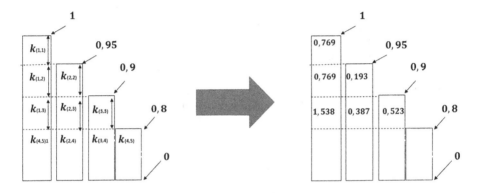

Fig. 8. k-bounding process for query Q_1 of Example 1

4.2 Threshold Pruning and Result Ranking

Once we have computed our k-bound K', we can set the local probability threshold τ to the maximum probability at site $K' + 1$ ($\tau = P_{max}(S_{K'+1})$). Hence, for each site that has not been pruned, we request all tuples with probability greater than τ. We then rank the candidate tuples sent by each local site. The full TDUD algorithm is depicted in Algorithm 2.

Example 5. Let us consider the query Q_1 of the previous example. Once the k-bound pruning has been performed, the list of candidate sites where Q_1 should be executed is $L_{Q_1} = \{S_2, S_1, S_3\}$. Next, the TDUD algorithm selects the probability threshold: $\tau = P_{max}(S_4) = 0.8$. On each site, only tuples whose probability is higher than τ are selected, i.e.: $S_1.t_3, S_2.t_8, S_2.t_6, S_2.t_7$ and $S_3.t_{11}$, as depicted in Table 1. Consequently, the number of transferred tuples to the query site is 5.

We note that, in this paper, we do not give any theoretical proofs to show that the not contacted nodes do don't contain the top-k result. We particularly concentrate in our approach in minimizing the transferred data between the coordinator node and the other distributed nodes. Hence, the next section shows that nodes that have no result, will not be accessed.

Table 1. Result of top-4 query: Q_1

(a) Local pruning			**(b)** Result ranking		
S_1	S_2	S_3	S_1	S_2	S_3
t_3	t_8	t_{11}	t_3	t_8	t_{11}
-	t_6	-	-	t_6	-
-	t_7	-			

5   Experiment Evaluation

We experimentally evaluate the performance of our proposed algorithm TDUD. The goal of the experiments is twofold: first, we study the effect of different parameters for the proposed algorithms and second, we compare the proposed algorithms with NAIV and DUTk algorithms to show the efficiency of the pruning phase. We have generated an uncertain relation *Farm* with three attributes (Fig. 1). The uncertain attribute *Illness* has 60 possible domain values ($|D| = 60$). The database is horizontally distributed over 50 nodes and each node contains more than 230 000 tuples.

The database is distributed horizontally in a way that ensures that not all categorical values appear in every node. The data sets follow two different distributions (1) a *pairwise* distribution where the probabilities for an illness are chosen randomly from [0,1] and (2) a *Zipf* distribution over probabilities with the default Skewness 1.2.

We measure the total communication cost in terms of the number of transferred tuples. Thus, we measure the response time as the time elapsed between sending the query from the query site and receiving all the responses in the query site. Each experiment is repeated 10 times in order to calculate an average time.

All experiments were conducted over 50 nodes on a virtual cluster where each node has an Intel Core TM processor CPU 3.40 GHZ with 8 GB RAM and is implemented in the R and C# language.

5.1   Efficiency of TDUD

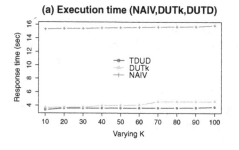
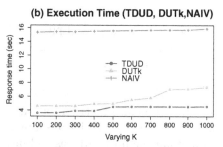

Fig. 9. Efficiency of TDUD with Pairwise Distribution by varying k

In this experiment, we empirically show the efficiency of the proposed TDUD algorithm. First, we consider the response time of TDUD compared with the naive one-round algorithm (NAIV) that sends all top-k tuples from each node to a central site and with the two-round algorithm, DUTk, proposed in [6]. In these experiments we varied the value of k. In Figs. 9(a) and 10(a), k is in the range $[10, 100]$ and for the (b) Figures it is in the range $[100, 1000]$. We observe that the TDUD algorithm entails linear computation time by increasing the size of k. For the highest value $k = 1000$, the total response time is about 3.65 s for TDUD and 5.49 s for DUTk.

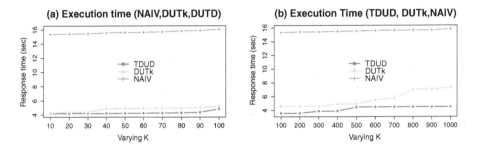

Fig. 10. Efficiency of TDUD with Zipf Distribution by varying k

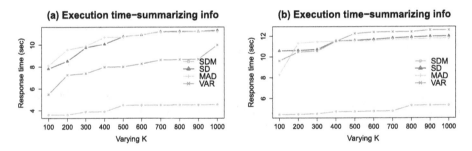

Fig. 11. Efficiency of TDUD with different summarizing information ((a) Pairwise Distribution, (b) Zipf)

In addition to NAIV and DUTk, we considered the use of the TDUD algorithm but with different summary statistics (namely the standard deviation (SD), mean absolute deviation(MAD), variance (VAR) and the statistic dispersion measure (SDM).

In this experiment, we varied k from 100 to 1000. The results are displayed in Fig. 11(a) (Pairwise Distribution) and Fig. 11(b) (Zipf Distribution). We clearly observe that the TDUD local summarizing measure gives better performance results than the provided classical measures.

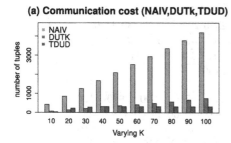

Fig. 12. TDUD with Pairwise Distribution

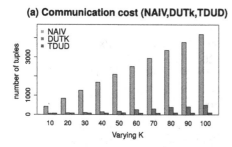
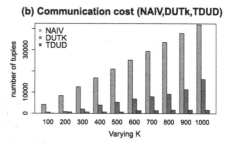

Fig. 13. TDUD with Zipf Distribution

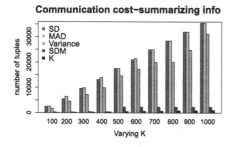
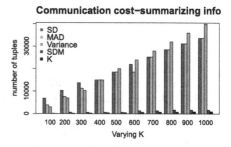

Fig. 14. Communication cost with different summarizing information ((a) Pairwise distribution, (b) Zipf Distribution)

5.2 Effectiveness of TDUD

We conducted experiments to show the effectiveness of TDUD in terms of communication cost, i.e. the number of transferred tuples from the distributed sites to the coordinator site. First, we consider the transfer of tuples of TDUD compared with the naive one-round algorithm that sends all top-k tuples from each node to a central site and with the two-round algorithm, DUTk, proposed in [6]. We varied the value of k. In Figs. 12(a) and 13(a), k is in the range [10, 100] for the (b) Figures, it is in the range [100, 1000].

k	10	20	30	40	50	60	70	80	90	100
NAIV	420	840	1260	1680	2100	2520	2940	3360	3780	4200
DUTk	65	134	211	316	361	417	480	567	666	753
TDUD	32	224	280	316	316	316	316	316	316	316

(a) $k \in \{10, 100\}$

k	100	200	300	400	500	600	700	800	900	1000
NAIV	4200	8400	12600	16800	2100	25200	29400	33600	37800	42000
DUTk	753	1656	2436	3556	4594	5343	6154	7479	8999	10348
TDUD	316	316	440	440	2269	2269	2269	2269	2269	2269

(b) $k \in \{100, 1000\}$

Fig. 15. Number of transferred tuples with Pairwise distribution

k	10	20	30	40	50	60	70	80	90	100
NAIV	420	840	1260	1680	2100	2520	2940	3360	3780	4200
DUTk	54	83	102	141	183	264	305	388	414	505
TDUD	68	77	77	77	100	20	20	103	103	105

(a) $k \in \{10, 100\}$

k	100	200	300	400	500	600	700	800	900	1000
NAIV	4200	8400	12600	16800	2100	25200	29400	33600	37800	42000
DUTk	507	856	2038	3922	5377	6963	7983	917	11383	16230
TDUD	105	655	655	655	655	1330	1330	1674	1674	1674

(b) $k \in \{100, 1000\}$

Fig. 16. Number of transferred tuples with Zipf distribution

In addition to NAIV and DUTk, we considered the use of the TDUD algorithm but with different summary statistics (namely the standard deviation (SD), mean absolute deviation (MAD), and variance (VAR). We compare this with the statistic dispersion measure (SDM) we propose in this paper (reported in the graphs as TDUD). In this experiment, we varied k from 100 to 1000. As shown in Figs. 14(a) and Fig. 14(b), with our proposed measure, the communication cost is much better than most of the classical measures except for SD. However, we show below that all these measures have higher error rates than TDUD (meaning they have lower recall and miss more of the actual top-k answers).

Figures 15 and 16 depict the number of tuples transferred using DUTk, TDUD and NAIV for the Pairwise and Zipf data sets respectively. As we see the number of tuples transferred using DUTk algorithm is greater than TDUD which means that TDUD algorithm significantly reduces an important number of transferred tuples that are not involved in the final result. The second important point observed in this experiment is that the number of tuples transferred using TDUD is always greater than the value of k which proves the exactness and correctness of our results. We note that smallest values of k DUTk gives a better performance.

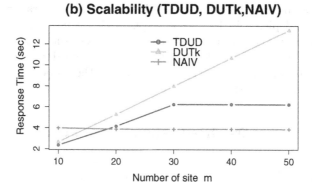

Fig. 17. Scalability of TDUD with Zipf Distribution by varying m and k = 400

5.3 Scalability

In this experiment, we study the scalability of our algorithm with respect to the number of distributed sites m.

We fix the size of the entire distributed data and vary the number of sites from 10 to 50. Figure 17 shows the results for fixed values of k = 400. DUTk and TDUD have good scalability w.r.t. the number of sites m and they outperform NAIV that increases linearly with m. we note that the gap between DUTk and TDUD compared to NAIV increases as m increases. This result is expected due to the fact that only a subset of sites are queried based on the GUI. Consequently, the number of sites does not effect the query processing. This clearly shows the benefit of only one round of communication on the scalability.

5.4 Data Shipment Overhead

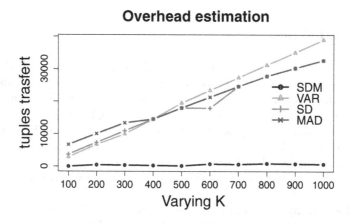

Fig. 18. Comparison of error estimation on tuples transfert varying the measure

In the last experiment, we studied the overhead estimation of transferring tuples. The results are depicted in Figs. 18 and 19. In this experiment, we study the response time by varying k the number of sites m and their size. We fixed the k-tuples to be calculated $k \in \{100, 500, 900\}$ and changed the number of sites $m \in \{10, 20, 30, 40, 50\}$. Figures 18 and 19 depict the response time of NAIV, DUTk, TDUD with increasing m.

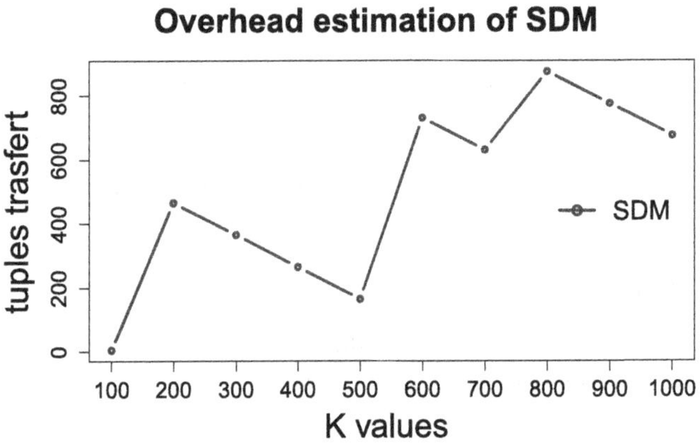

Fig. 19. Error estimation on tuples transfert of SDM

The results show that when k is small the performances of DUTk, TDUD are approximately the same (Fig. 18 and 19). While TDUD outperforms the other two approaches when k is high, its response time is affected very little with increasing m. The algorithm TDUD reaches its fixed point as shown in Fig. 18. This result is expected due to the fact that given a value of k, only a subset of sites are queried based on the GUI. Consequently, the number of sites does not effect the query processing.

6   Related Work

There has been significant work on uncertain data management lately due to the emergence of many applications which naturally create uncertain information in domains that include sensor networks, data cleaning, and location tracking. Some of the most investigated topics are modeling [5,10] and processing [9,18] uncertain data. Many query processing techniques have been studied, with much interest in top-k queries. The definitions and semantics of top-k uncertain queries have been presented in detail [13,14]. Existing work on top-k query processing over uncertain data however considers mainly centralized environments [9,12, 20,24].

Nowadays, many applications where uncertainty arises are distributed in nature, e.g., distributed sensor networks, distributed integration of information from multiple sources, etc. However, existing techniques including indexing and query processing over uncertain data for centralized data are not adaptable to distributed environments. As a result, it is still a challenging issue to efficiently process queries over distributed uncertain data. Existing work on distributed uncertain data were mainly applied for skyline queries [16,17], wireless sensor networks [23].

The most relevant work to this paper are on top-k queries over distributed uncertain data, starting from the work of Li and colleagues [15], where they proposed an algorithm using the notion of expected rank to retrieve the top-k tuples with the lowest ranks from distributed sites. They demonstrated how to alleviate the computational burden at distributed sites so that high communication and computation efficiency are achieved simultaneously. However, the main drawback is the transmission bandwidth trading-off latency.

Sun and colleagues [9] studied top-k query on uncertain data across P2P networks. They proposed a global Q-tree index based on a Q-tree structure. The global index summarizes all indices of peers in the P2P network, where each peer has a local index based on the same structure of the global index. This approach deals with uncertain objects, however, the main algorithm requires several rounds of communication between the peers in the network. Another work relevant to this paper is AbdulAzeem et al. [1], proposed a framework for ranking distributed uncertain data, based on three layers: query, ranking and monitoring. The drawback of this work is the transmission bandwidth at the ranking layer that results from distributed nodes sending all their promising tuples to the query node, even if they do not contribute to the final result.

To the best of our knowledge, our work is the first to address the problem of processing top-k queries over distributed uncertain categorical data in only one round of communication that uses summary statistics to estimate if fewer than k tuples can be retrieve from a node and to prune (and not contact) nodes that are unlikely to contain any top-k answers.

7   Conclusion

This work introduces a new algorithm for top-k query processing in uncertain distributed databases that improves the state of the art. In particular, we focused on indexing techniques for categorical uncertain data. We introduced a statistical dispersion measure that is stored in a global index to summarize the probability distributions of information in local indexes. We use the dispersion measure to estimate if fewer than k tuples can be retrieved from a node and to prune (and not contact) nodes that are unlikely to contain any top-k answers. The algorithm was shown to have good scalability with the respect to the number of nodes. Experimental results showed that the algorithm performed efficiently in response time as well as the communication cost.

In future work, we shall consider the extension of indexing techniques for more general uncertain attributes and richer query semantics. Hence, we will experimentally demonstrates our approach on real dataset

Acknowledgements. We thank and show our gratitude to Salima Benbernou and Renée Miller for relevant and helpful comments and suggestions that greatly improved the manuscript.

References

1. AbdulAzeem, Y.M., El-Desouky, A.I., Ali, H.A.: A framework for ranking uncertain distributed database. Data Knowl. Eng. **92**, 1–19 (2014)
2. AbdulAzeem, Y.M., Eldesouky, A.I., Ali, H.A., Salem, M.M.: Ranking distributed database in tuple-level uncertainty. Soft Comput. **19**(4), 965–980 (2014). https://doi.org/10.1007/s00500-014-1306-9
3. Agarwal, P.K., Cheng, S., Tao, Y., Yi, K.: Indexing uncertain data. In: PODS (2009)
4. Amagata, D., Sasaki, Y., Hara, T., Nishio, S.: Probabilistic nearest neighbor query processing on distributed uncertain data. Distrib. Parallel Databases **34**(2), 259–287 (2015). https://doi.org/10.1007/s10619-015-7183-0
5. Barbará, D., Garcia-Molina, H., Porter, D.: The management of probabilistic data. IEEE Trans. Knowl. Data Eng. **4**(5), 487–502 (1992)
6. Benaissa, A., Benbernou, S., Ouziri, M., Sahri, S.: Indexing uncertain categorical data over distributed environment. In: IFSA-EUSFLAT (2015)
7. Benaissa, A., Yahmi, M., Jamil, Y.: Framework for managing uncertain distributed categorical data. Int. J. Adv. Comput. Sci. Appl. **8**(10), 359 (2017)
8. Cavallo, R., Pittarelli, M.: The theory of probabilistic databases. In: VLDB (1987)
9. Cheng, R., Xia, Y., Prabhakar, S., Shah, R., Vitter, J.S.: Efficient indexing methods for probabilistic threshold queries over uncertain data. In: VLDB (2004)
10. Dalvi, N.N., Suciu, D.: Efficient query evaluation on probabilistic databases. In: VLDB (2004)
11. Fang, Q., Yang, G.: Efficient top-k query processing algorithms in highly distributed environments. JCP **9**(9), 2000–2006 (2014)
12. Hua, M., Pei, J., Zhang, W., Lin, X.: Ranking queries on uncertain data: a probabilistic threshold approach. In: SIGMOD (2008)
13. Ilyas, I.F., Beskales, G., Soliman, M.A.: A survey of top-k query processing techniques in relational database systems. ACM Comput. Surv. **40**(4), 1–58 (2008)
14. Jestes, J., Cormode, G., Li, F., Yi, K.: Semantics of ranking queries for probabilistic data. IEEE Trans. Knowl. Data Eng. **23**(12), 1903–1917 (2011)
15. Li, F., Yi, K., Jestes, J.: Ranking distributed probabilistic data. In: SIGMOD Conference (2009)
16. Li, X., Wang, Y., Li, X., Wang, X., Yu, J.: GDPS: an efficient approach for skyline queries over distributed uncertain data. Big Data Res. **1**, 23–36 (2014)
17. Li, X., Wang, Y., Yu, J.: An efficient scheme for probabilistic skyline queries over distributed uncertain data. Telecommun. Syst. **60**(2), 225–237 (2015). https://doi.org/10.1007/s11235-015-0025-6
18. Singh, S., Mayfield, C., Prabhakar, S., Shah, R., Hambrusch, S.E.: Indexing uncertain categorical data. In: ICDE (2007)
19. Soliman, M.A., Ilyas, I.F., Chang, K.C.: Top-k query processing in uncertain databases. In: ICDE (2007)
20. Soliman, M.A., Ilyas, I.F., Chang, K.C.: URank: formulation and efficient evaluation of top-k queries in uncertain databases. In: SIGMOD (2007)

21. Sun, Y., Yuan, Y., Wang, G.: Top-k query processing over uncertain data indistributed environments. World Wide Web **15**, 429–446 (2012). https://doi.org/10.1007/s11280-011-0141-5
22. Wang, X., Shen, D., Yu, G.: Uncertain top-k query processing in distributedenvironments. Distrib. Parallel Databases **34**(4), 567–589 (2016)
23. Ye, M., Liu, X., Lee, W., Lee, D.L.: Probabilistic top-k query processing in distributed sensor networks. In: ICDE (2010)
24. Yi, K., Li, F., Kollios, G., Srivastava, D.: Efficient processing of top-k queries in uncertain databases. In: ICDE (2008)

On Knowledge Transfer from Cost-Based Optimization of Data-Centric Workflows to Business Process Redesign

Georgia Kougka[1], Konstantinos Varvoutas[1], Anastasios Gounaris[1($\boxtimes$)], George Tsakalidis[2], and Kostas Vergidis[2]

[1] Department of Informatics, Aristotle University of Thessaloniki, Thessaloniki, Greece
{georkoug,kmvarvou,gounaria}@csd.auth.gr
[2] Department of Applied Informatics, University of Macedonia, Thessaloniki, Greece
{giorgos.tsakalidis,kvergidis}@uom.edu.gr

Abstract. This work deals with redesigning business process models, e.g., in BPMN, based on cost-based optimization techniques that were initially proposed for data analytics workflows. More specifically, it discusses execution cost and cycle time improvements through treating business processes in the same way as data-centric workflows. The presented solutions are cost-based, i.e., they employ quantitative metadata and cost models. The advantage of this approach is that business processes can benefit from recent advances in data-intensive workflow optimization similarly to the manner they nowadays benefit from additional data analytics areas, e.g., in the area of process mining. Concrete use cases are presented that are capable of demonstrating that even in small, more conservative cases, the benefits are significant. The contribution of this work is to show how to automatically optimize the model structure of a given process in terms of the ordering of tasks and how to perform resource allocation under contradicting objectives. Finally, the work identifies open issues in developing end-to-end business process redesign solutions with regards to the case studies considered.

1 Introduction

Modern *Business Processes (BPs)* constitute a key part of businesses and their modeling, execution and evolution are critical aspects in *Business Process Management (BPM)*. The BPM is defined as a body of methods, techniques and tools to discover, analyze, redesign, execute and monitor these business processes [17]. In such a context, a fundamental role of BPM is to adapt business functions to the requirements of each business's customer, allocate efficiently the business resources, target at both improving the quality of services delivered while keeping the cost low, keep the processes as simple and flexible as possible, and so on. In order to fulfill these demanding and often contradicting business requirements, the behavior of business processes is closely monitored after their

© Springer-Verlag GmbH Germany, part of Springer Nature 2020
A. Hameurlain and A Min Tjoa (Eds.): TLDKS XLIII, LNCS 12130, pp. 62–85, 2020.
https://doi.org/10.1007/978-3-662-62199-8_3

deployment, so as to gain insights that were unknown at design time. Such information can be used for adapting the process's design to improve if not optimize its efficiency.

The optimization of the BPs, as considered in this work, refers to (incremental) BP *redesign*, which is an essential part of BPM lifecycle and a necessary action to ensure the best schedule, coordination and execution of business activities [23]. We assume that it is trivial to design an initial BP model, which is then frequently refined to optimize certain metrics and/or adapt to changing conditions. The re-ordering of the BPs's tasks and re-allocation of the available resources are key examples of BP optimization actions. Nevertheless, up to date, these optimization actions are applied mostly manually based on the experience of the business users and the help of BPMN software tools [1–4], which do not support fully-automated optimization solutions and require human interaction. Consequently, there is a demanding need to introduce automated optimization solutions, where automation covers not only the monitoring of the process and the identification of an issue but also the modification of the process model structure, such as changing the order in which tasks are placed in the model and executed. The aim of this work is to introduce techniques for automated BP optimization inspired by a set of well-investigated algorithms proposed for data-centric workflow optimization [26,27,30]. This is aligned to several recent attempts to further blend advanced data analytics with business processes [44]. More specifically, in this work, it is demonstrated how to automatically optimize the task ordering, thus modifying the model structure of a given process, and how to perform resource allocation under contradicting objectives.

BP redesign is a well investigated area; nevertheless, it is mostly based on heuristics (see Appendix in [17] for a complete list) with a lack of automated optimization solutions [52] that can be directly run on initial model structures. BP redesign covers both evolutionary and revolutionary approaches (see Ch. 8 in [17]); our work fits better the evolutionary paradigm, where we restructure an existing process model or we perform resource allocation in an informed manner. Cost-based optimization solutions for BPs have been explored but they are incomplete from the algorithmic point of view and inferior to those in the area of optimization of data-centric workflows [29,42]. An example that we particularly deal with in this work concerns ordering knock-out tasks, i.e., tasks that may lead to immediate process termination; in this context, to minimize total cost, the underpinnings of the works in [5] (regarding BPs) and [26] (regarding workflows for data analytics) are the same; however, the latter goes one step beyond and provides a more complete algorithmic solution in that it takes into account a broader range of workflows containing additional tasks apart from knock-out ones and arbitrary dependency constraints between them, as is the norm.

Before delving into details, it is important to distinguish between the meaning of the term "data flow" in the different communities. In the broader data-management community, data flows denote data-centric workflows, e.g., as supported by modern tools, such as Apache Spark [55]. However, in business processes, data flow is used as complementary to control flow: the former emphasizes on the artifacts, such as documents, required to perform a task, whereas the latter indicates when tasks and events should occur [17]. Our work advocates leveraging advances in data-centric workflows to optimize the control flow of BPs; optimizing the data flow in BPs. e.g., as in [25], is a complementary area to our proposal.

The optimization of BPs may consider multiple critical objectives, such as the minimization of the economic and time cost ensuring that the quality of service is high. Other examples of optimization objectives are the response time and the resource utilization. Similarly, the means to improve on these metrics vary: from dropping unnecessary tasks to reordering tasks and modifying the resource allocation. In this work, we will focus on automated BP optimization considering multi-criteria improvement, such as the minimization of execution cost and cycle time of BPs using a principled approach to investigating alternative task orderings and task allocation solutions. The contribution of this work is to present complete solutions and anticipated benefits to the problem of reordering knock-out tasks and modifying the allocated resources to business processes, and finally, understanding better the issues involved in coupling BP redesign and data-centric workflow optimization more tightly.

The structure of the manuscript is described as follows. We present the related work of optimizing BPMN processes in Sect. 2. We describe motivational examples in order to highlight the need for adopting cost-based optimization solutions in Sect. 3. The metadata definition and the necessary background for applying the optimization algorithms, along with the optimization metrics are presented in Sect. 4. The next section shows how knock-out processes can be treated in a principled manner and provides insights into the expected benefits in a real scenario; in addition, we provide an approach to bi-objective optimization using another real scenario. Software implementation issues are treated in Sect. 6 along with a detailed discussion of open issues, whereas the following section concludes this work.

2   Related Work

Several optimization techniques to support BP redesign have been proposed. For example, the authors in [17] summarize all the heuristics in order to refine an existing process or eliminate redundant tasks by merging or removing processes (without presenting concrete algorithms). Similarly, good practices, such as using as few elements in the model as possible and employing models as structured as possible avoiding OR routing elements appear in [34]. Similarly, the work in [18] advocates following high-level business process improvement patterns. Another redesign approach is to exploit queue theory to emulate human or machines that execute tasks [15] with a view to driving decisions regarding task re-ordering, resource allocation and task implementation. Contrary to the use cases we consider, the focus of the work in [15] is on how to merge different tasks into groups that can be handled by the same team of actors. Additionally, there are proposals considering variant optimization objectives, such as the techniques in [5], where a set of heuristics is introduced for optimizing the metrics of resource utilization, maximal throughput and execution (cycle) time. These heuristics consider changing the relative ordering of tasks, enforcing parallel execution and task merging; essentially, they constitute building blocks for developing automated algorithms rather than proposing full algorithms. Finally, another interesting approach to redesigning BPs is the re-configuration of the BP models that comprise several variants, e.g. so that different tokens in the same BPMN flow may follow different paths as proposed in [32].

Regarding data-centric workflows, a lot of effort is towards finding the best sequential order of flow tasks [26,27] to minimize the sum of the costs of these tasks. Another important optimization mechanism examined in the state-of-the-art is the selection of the best execution option of a process, choosing between multiple human and/or physical resources/alternatives [30]. Additionally, there are proposals that optimize different single objectives than the sum of the costs, such as the improvement of the sum of the task costs of the critical flow execution path [8] or the task ordering to maximize the utilization of each execution processor [16]. All these proposals aim to optimize a single criterion, but there are also proposals that target multi-objective data flow optimization, such as the algorithms in [46,47] that consider the sum of the task costs along with the reliability, in the form of fault tolerance.

In addition, there are several recent proposals on data analytics-driven solutions for BPM problems. Examples include process mining and discovery, e.g., [7,9,10,56], and querying-based [40] process enhancements. Process mining in particular is both orthogonal and complementary to our research. More specifically, process mining may be used to extract the necessary statistical metadata, e.g., [6] (Ch. 8.4) and precedence constraints, e.g., [41,48] to be presented in the next sections, but this direction is not covered in this work.

A significant part of recent research in BPs targets variability between process models aiming at the same high-level objectives [45,54]. For example, the work in [45] is motivated from the fact that the same goal in different municipalities is performed using different equivalent processes and, to manage such variability, it introduces the configurable process trees. This methodology allows a specific set of process models to be selected according to several criteria. The main difference with our work is that we explore process model alternatives that are not known a-priori where the search space may be exponential, e.g. when examining the ordering of knock-out tasks for which any ordering is valid. In such a context, proposals like [14] deal with the problem of extracting alternative models, whereas the issue of assessing the quality of different process model configurations [13] and quantifying the differences between process models [11] have also been explored. Finally, our work relates to declarative process models [33,37,38]; e.g., our task ordering solution can be seen as a promising means to derive executable model structures out of such declarative models.

3   Targeted Use Cases

This section presents the use cases we primarily target.

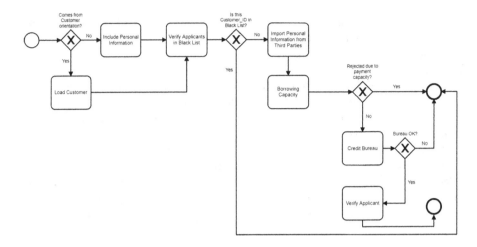

Fig. 1. A model representing a loan verification procedure.

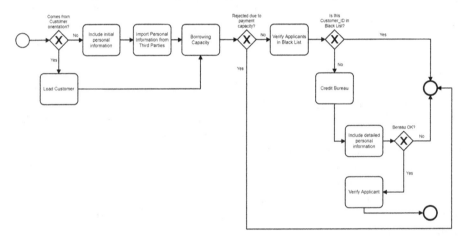

Fig. 2. Task decomposition and re-ordering examples in a business process in BPMN in Fig. 1.

3.1 Loan Application

In Fig. 1, we show a BP example of a typical bank loan application processing. This BP consists of seven tasks, namely and two start/end events. These tasks include three checks (*Verify Applicants in Black List, Borrowing Capacity, Credit Bureau*) and a final verification phase. The checks, according to the outcome of which the loan application proceeds or is rejected, are typical examples of knock-out tasks in the sense that if the application does not pass them, the process terminates.

Assume that the second knock-out task, i.e., the one referring to the borrowing capacity, is much more selective than the first one, i.e., the one referring to the

Table 1. The dependency constraints of the BPMN scenario of Fig. 2.

Task preceding	Task succeeding
Include initial personal information or load customer	Verify applicants in black list, import personal info from third parties, borrowing capacity, credit bureau, verify applicant
Import personal information from third parties	Borrowing capacity, credit bureau
Verify applicants in black list, borrowing capacity, credit bureau	Verify application

black list; in such a case, it is beneficial to swap the first two checks. The interesting part is that, in order to run the second check, another task, namely *Import Personal Information from Third Parties*, is required to be moved upstream as well. Let us further assume that in this scenario, the checks are automated and each one takes less than 1 min to complete, whereas an employee requires 25 min per customer in order to fill all the necessary forms with the personal details of a customer (*Include Personal Information*). This implies that the complete BP execution delays, until this task is completed while, in case of application rejection, not all the info is needed. Therefore, one can reduce the cycle time through (i) decomposing the complex task of *Include Personal Information* to two simpler tasks, only the first of which is required to run the subsequent three checks; (ii) moving the non-necessary part of the detailed application information either after all knock-out tasks or in parallel with them; an example is shown in Fig. 2. Such re-ordering and/or decomposition optimization actions can yield improvements regarding both the resource consumption and the process cycle time.

A main question that arises is as to whether we can be sure that the semantics of the process have not been modified and re-ordering tasks does not affect the rationale of the process. To ensure these requirements, we need to respect the precedence (or dependency) constraints between tasks. These constraints for the running example are shown in Table 1, and they should be interpreted as follows: in any path from a source event to an end event that contains tasks in the same row of the table, the tasks in the left column should be placed beforehand the ones in the right column. In other words, in each row, the tasks in the right cell depend on the output of the tasks in the left cell. Therefore, we use the terms dependency and precedence constraints interchangeably in this work.

The contents of Table 1 can be represented as a graph with an edge starting from a task in the left cell pointing to a task in the right cell in the same row. The full list of the precedence constraints is derived from the transitive closure in such a graph. These constraints can be derived manually with the help of process analysts and domain experts; automated extraction, even in data-centric

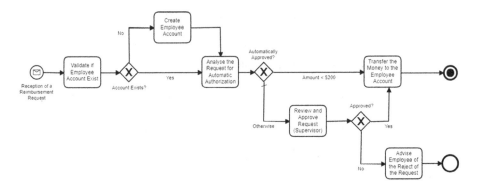

Fig. 3. Another business process model example that is amenable to optimizations.

workflows, is still not a mature area [42].[1] In this case study, we assume that the process designer also provides the constraints; issues related to constraints are further discussed in Sect. 6.

3.2 Reimbursement Request

An additional motivational example is presented in Fig. 3, where we show a BP example of an *Employee Expense Reimbursement Request* process[2]. This BP consists of six tasks that are required to validate, analyse, approve and pay an expense statement submitted by an employee of a business. Despite its simplicity and the fact that there are no knock-out tasks, this process is also amenable to optimizations regarding the cycle time. For example, if the bottleneck is the review from a supervisor for amounts larger than $200, then more resources can be allocated to this task leading to a trade-off regarding cycle time and resource consumption (and monetary cost). In addition, we can move the supervisor review in parallel with the account existence check to save time. The goal is to employ automated solutions that explore all such alternatives.

4   Definitions and Optimization Objectives

We consider a BP to be a sextuple $P = (V, G, E, A, I, O)$, where V is the non-empty set of tasks, G is the set of gateways, E the set of edges connecting the tasks and the gateways, A is the set of actors executing the tasks, I is the set of input events, and O is the output events.

We restrict ourselves to a subset of BPMN elements, comprising simple, loop, multiple instance, compensation and adhoc tasks, (event) subprocesses,

---

[1] Note that these constraints refer to the process model structure; additional execution constraints, e.g., two tasks share the same resource and thus cannot run simultaneously, affect the cost models that quantify the optimization objectives (see also Sect. 4.2).

[2] taken from https://www.businessprocessincubator.com/.

AND/OR/XOR-splits, and start, end and wait timer events (wait timer events are considered as an annotation to edges). For all these elements, a mapping to a DAG (directed acyclic graph) is possible [19], even when cycles and loops exist in the model. Working with a subset of BPMN elements is common, e.g., as in [22,43], to reduce the complexity of the proposed techniques. We consider both well-structured processes [24], e.g., derived through the process in [39] and unstructured ones. Re-sequencing is inherently more suitable for unstructured BPs containing knock-out tasks; because knock-out tasks are followed by splits, a branch of which can lead to immediate termination. On the other hand, parallelizing blocks of tasks and choosing their implementations benefits more from structured processes in our cases. Finally, note that elements, such as BPMN data objects, need not appear in the BPMN diagrams.

4.1 Processes as Annotated DAGs

We map processes P to a DAG $P' = (V', E')$, where $V' \supseteq V$ and $E' = (v'_i, v'_j)$, $v'_i, v'_j \in V'$ (E' is neither a subset nor a superset of E). P' is annotated and more specifically, in our techniques in the next subsections, we require two quantitative metadata types for each vertex in P' in addition to the precedence constraints:

- *Cost* (c_i) per input token defines the cost of a task v'_i, $v'_i \in V'$, $i = 1 \dots |V'|$ to process a token. The cost can be either in time or in actual monetary cost units.
- *Selectivity* (sel_i) defines the (average) ratio of the output to the input tokens of v'_i. In many cases, the selectivity is 1, but lower selectivity values denote knock-out processes and/or are used to define the fraction of token flow after non-parallel gateways.

For the mapping purposes, we introduce the term *dummy tasks* [19]. These tasks represent artificial tasks that are characterized with appropriate statistical metadata to represent the flow of a BP. Finally, note that the edges in E' denote token flow exclusively.

Figures 4 and 5 show the corresponding DAG representations of each of the scenarios in Figs. 1 and 3, respectively following the methodology in [19]. In the figures, we use example metadata. For instance, in Fig. 4, the three checks have selectivity values 0.6, 0.8 and 0.5, respectively, whereas only 70% of the application that pass through these checks are finally approved. For the *Reimbursement Request* case study, the *Analyze Request* task has selectivity > 1, to account for the fact that a request may contain more than one separate claims.

4.2 Optimizations Objectives

Cost-based optimization heavily relies on amortized metrics across several process instantiations. It is also helpful to define the *input* (inp_i) of a task. More specifically, inp_i defines the size input of the v'_i in number of tokens. If v'_i

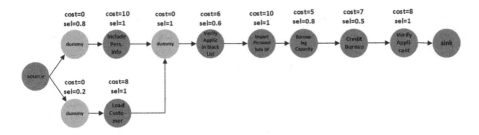

Fig. 4. A DAG representation of the model in Fig. 1.

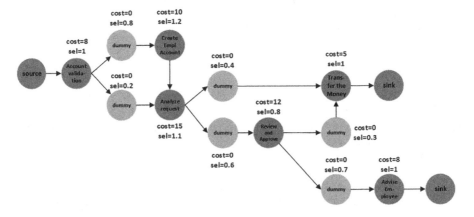

Fig. 5. A DAG representation of the model in Fig. 3.

receives input only from v'_j, then $inp_i = inp_j * sel_j$. In the generic case, $inp_i = \sum_{(v'_j, v'_i) \in E'} inp_j * sel_j$. In any case, inp_i depends on the product of the selectivities of the preceding tasks in the same path/branch in P'.

We consider the following two optimization objectives, which are common in BPs [17] (Ch. 7):

- *Monetary Cost/Resource Consumption* is defined by the human and machine costs. The human cost reflects the human resource consumption required to complete a BP execution, while the machine cost reflects the other resources that are necessary for the BP execution. This type of cost, given a set of tasks V' with known cost and selectivity values, is defined as follows:

$$Cost = \sum_{i=1}^{|V'|} c_i * inp_i$$

When c_i is in time units, the formula above computes the total time resources are occupied. If the cost is in monetary cost units, the formula computes the expenses associated with such resource usage.

- *Cycle time* represents the average time between the start of a process execution and its completion time. Generally, we define the cycle time as the sum of the costs of the tasks that belong to the critical path of a BP. The critical path is a path from a source to an end that takes the longest to complete. Taking the sum of the costs covers a wide range of cases, e.g., a model in the form of a chain, where each task is activated upon the receipt of a token, i.e., there are no waiting times or the (amortized) waiting times are included in task costs. If all tasks are executed by the same resource, then we need to sum the costs of all tasks, not only those in the critical path, to reflect the fact that tasks cannot be executed simultaneously.

5 Optimization Solutions

In this section, we provide algorithmic details and evaluation results regarding the two main problems we target in this work, namely reordering tasks in process models that contain knock-out tasks and treating bi-objective solutions regarding resource allocation in a principled manner.

5.1 Reordering Knock-Out Tasks

First, we deal with reordering DAGs corresponding to BPs that contain knock-out tasks, i.e., tasks with selectivity not always set to 1 capitalizing on the state-of-art in data-centric workflow optimization, as the latter is presented in [29, 42]. Given the existence of efficient techniques for optimizing chains of tasks in data-centric workflows, the idea is to extract source-to-end linear segments (i.e., paths) corresponding to branches with knock-out tasks and then, optimize the extracted paths using existing techniques. In other words, given also that the problem is NP-hard [29], we follow a divide-and-conquer approach dealing with smaller parts of the DAG in each step to strike an acceptable balance between optimization overhead and solution optimality.

The important issue is that other types of tasks, i.e., non-selective ones, can exist as well. Let the *rank* value of a task be $\frac{1-sel_i}{c_i}$. It is well-known that ranking knock-out tasks according to their *rank* values yields an optimal solution in terms of the sum of the costs [5], but such an ordering is not always feasible due to precedence constraints. Therefore, more complete algorithms that build upon this principle have been developed with the proposals in [26] claiming to be the most advanced solutions to date. In addition, although the whole ordering can be done in several manners in polynomial time, for isolated paths with not a high number of tasks, exhaustive solutions are applicable in practice due to the efficient handling of the precedence constraints, as thoroughly discussed in [27]. A strong point of this approach is that the final ordering relies on the statistical metadata and precedence constraints rather than any initial designer decisions. More specifically, for a given linear segment, the initial ordering plays no role.

Solution Details. The solution is outlined in Algorithm 1. This algorithm is a hybrid one and, as shown in line 2, defines the specific algorithm to be applied based on the properties of the path extracted. If the number of tasks

---

Algorithm 1. ReorderingBPs

1: Extract the largest source-to-end linear segment (path) from the DAG containing tasks with selectivity lower than 1.
2: **if** path size is shorter than (15 tasks) OR (shorter than 30 and DoF < 0.1) **then**
3:     execute Algorithm 2
4: **else**
5:     execute Algorithm 3
6: **end if**
7: remove all tasks in the selected path from the DAG and if there still exist tasks with selectivity <1 go to Step 1

Algorithm 2. TopSort (exact algorithm taken from [27])

Require: 1. A set of n tasks, T=$\{t_1, ..., t_n\}$.
            2. A directed acyclic graph PC of precedence constraints.
            3. A function computeCost (the one in Section 4.2 can be used)
Ensure: An ordering of the tasks P representing the optimal plan.
1: P=$\{t_1, t_2, ..., t_n\}$ {P is initialized with a valid topological ordering of PC.}
2: i←1
3: minCost ← computeCost(P)
4: **while** $i < n$ {n is the total number of tasks} **do**
5:     k ← location of t_i in P
6:     k1 ← k + 1
7:     **if** $P(k1)$ task has prerequisite t_i **then**
8:         // **Rotation stage**
9:         Rotate the elements of P from positions i to k
10:         cost ← computeCost(P)
11:         i← i+1
12:     **else**
13:         // **Swapping stage**
14:         Swap the k and $k1$ elements of P
15:         cost ← computeCost(P)
16:         i ← 1
17:     **end if**
18:     **if** cost < minCost **then**
19:         bestP ← P
20:         minCost ← cost
21:     **end if**
22: **end while**
23: P ← bestP

---

in the extracted path is less than 15 or it is less than thirty with low task re-ordering flexibility, then the exact algorithm in Algorithm 2 is applied; otherwise we resort to a fast yet approximate solution (Algorithm 3). Later, we present experiments to explain the choice of these parameters. The flexibility in the ordering of the tasks is quantified with the help of the *DoF* (Degree-of-Freedom) metric. For a path with n tasks, when there is only a single alternative for task ordering, the corresponding transitive closure of the graph representing

Algorithm 3. RO-III (approximate algorithm taken from [26])

Require: A set of n tasks, T={t_1, ..., t_n}
    A directed acyclic graph PC of precedence constraints
Ensure: A directed acyclic graph P representing the optimal plan
 1: Find paths in PC sharing source and sink vertices
 2: Extract the innermost and most upstream set of paths with common sink and
    sources
 3: $PC \leftarrow$ merge all such paths in a common path according to their rank value
 4: Go to Step 1 until there are no other such paths in the modified PC
 5: $G \leftarrow$ Apply KBZ algorithm [31] given the modified precedence constraints
 6: **repeat**
 7:    {k is the maximum subplan size considered}
 8:    **for** i←1:k **do**
 9:      **for** s←1:n-i **do**
10:        **for** t←s+i:n **do**
11:          consider moving subplan of size i starting from the sth task after the tth
           task in G
12:        **end for**
13:      **end for**
14:    **end for**
15: **until** no changes applied
16: P ← G

the precedence constraints has $n_{fullPCedges} = \frac{n(n-1)}{2}$ edges. Let $n_{PCedges}$ be the edges in the transitive closure of the precedence constraint graph. Then, $DoF = 1 - \frac{n_{PCedges}}{n_{fullPCedges}}$. Values closer to 1 denote maximum flexibility, e.g., as in the ad-hoc BPMN sub-processes, while values closer to 0 denote existence of few ordering alternatives.

Algorithm 2 presents the *TopSort* algorithm from [27] and is based on the solution from [51], which finds all the possible topological sortings given a partial ordering of a finite set. The algorithm is, by the problem definition, exponential in the worst case due to the size of the output (i.e., to enumerate all orderings), but, as will be shown, it is particularly useful in cases where the longest path of tasks does not comprise many tasks or there are highly restrictive precedence constraints. For the remaining cases, the authors advocate using Algorithm 3 from [26], termed as *ROIII*. This algorithm first renders the DAG applicable to a well-known optimization solution [21,31] for database queries since the 80s, namely the so-called KBZ algorithm that was initially proposed for join ordering. This is done through manipulating the precedence constraints graph (lines 1–4) but comes at the expense of missing optimization opportunities. To ameliorate the latter drawback, the algorithm performs a heuristic post-processing step (lines 6–16). Overall, its complexity is $O(n^3)$ and for small k values in Algorithm 3, it becomes quadratic [26].

To explain the switch condition in line 2 of Algorithm 1, the scalability of the exact and approximate algorithms need to be examined. In the experiments, a i7-4770 CPU at 3.4 GHz with 16 GB of RAM was used. As shown in Fig. 6,

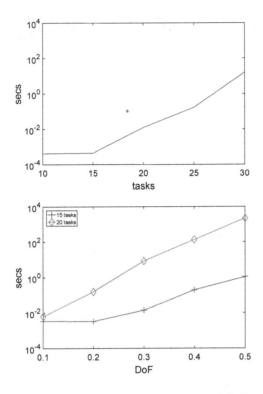

Fig. 6. TopSort scalability for varying number of tasks and DoF set to 0.1 (top) and varying DoF for 15 and 20 tasks (bottom).

the optimization overhead of *TopSort* grows significantly when the number of tasks exceeds 15, unless the *DoF* is kept low (< 0.1) where the tasks can be up to 30 and the optimization overhead is kept under 1 min. For *TopSort*, the *DoF* value is important because it defines how many plans need to be checked. On the other hand, *ROIII* is more insensitive to the *DoF* value and even for 100 tasks, it runs in under a second (see Fig. 7).

Example Benefits. In order to assess the potential benefits of such re-ordering, we run the following experiment. The purpose of this experiment is to show that even in more conservative cases, the benefits are significant. More specifically, we consider two simple processes with just two and three knock-out tasks, respectively. For each task, the cost and the selectivity varies uniformly in the range [0.1, 1], which means that the costlier (resp. most selective) case differs from the less expensive (resp. less selective) by an order of magnitude; there are also start and end tasks with cost equal to the lowest of the knock-out ones (i.e., 0.1). The results are shown in Fig. 8, where for each range of improvement values, we can see the probability of occurrence. When there are only two knock-out tasks, in 12% of the cases, the unoptimized plan has higher cost and cycle time by

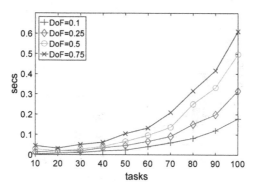

Fig. 7. ROIII scalability for varying number of tasks and DoF values.

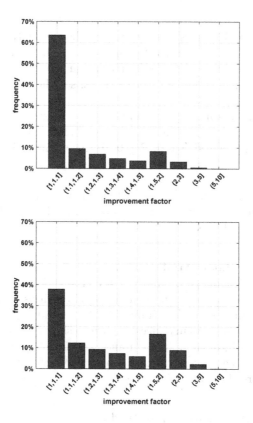

Fig. 8. Histograms regarding how many times the unoptimized process is slower than the optimized one when the process comprises solely two (top) and three (bottom) knock-out tasks.

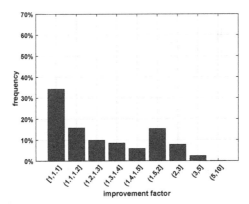

Fig. 9. Histogram regarding how many times the unoptimized process is slower than the optimized one when the process comprises four knock-out tasks with precedence constraints.

50% and more (up to 3.9 times), as denoted by the cumulative frequency of the four rightmost bars in Fig. 8 (top). When there are three knock-out tasks, the non-optimized processes are inferior by more than 50% in 27.5% of the cases; the highest improvement observed is 6.79 times; see the four rightmost bars in Fig. 8 (bottom).

Next, we slightly modify the setting above as follows: we increase the number of tasks to four, but between 2 random pairs we enforce precedence constraints. The resulting histogram is shown in Fig. 9. In this scenario, in 25% of the cases, the unnecessary overhead is higher than 50%. In the worst case, it is 5.68 times higher.

The benefits over a random initial ordering can grow arbitrarily large, if we consider more knock-out tasks within a process, with larger differences between the extremum cost and selectivity values.

Application to the Loan Application. We apply the proposed technique to the load application scenario, where there are three knock-out tasks along with several other ones. We allow the costs and the selectivities of the tasks to differ by an order of magnitude at most (ranges [1, 10] and [0.1, 1], respectively) and we run 10000 random process instances. Figure 10 shows the speed-ups when the non-knock-out tasks have the minimum and the maximum costs. In the former case, the optimized plan is less expensive by up to 3.86 times and the benefits exceed 20% in more than 40% of the cases.

5.2   Dealing with Optimization Trade-Offs

In the previous task re-ordering example, we essentially manipulate the set E of the BP edges. Next, we shift our attention to the properties of actors A, where we assume that the mapping of tasks to actors is already given through a

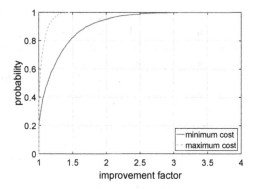

Fig. 10. The cumulative distribution function of the times of improvement for the loan application use case.

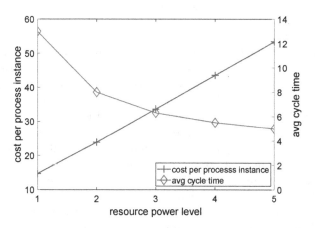

Fig. 11. Cost vs cycle-time trade-off example.

function f, s.t. $f(V) \rightarrow A$. We are motivated by the fact that cycle time and cost are often contradictory objectives. For example, consider the scenario in Fig. 3, where we assume that all tasks have cost equal to 1 cost unit and take 1 time unit to complete, apart from the review task that is 10 times costlier and more time consuming, and is allocated to a different actor. Further assume that we monitor the average performance across 100 input tokens (with 10 time units time gap between two instances). All requests are above \$200 and approved.

Figure 11 shows the trade-off between cost and cycle-time when we increase the power of the bottleneck actor 2, 3, 4 and 5 times. When we double the power of the resource, the cost doubles and the time spent drops to the half. The results are derived using the BIMP simulator [2]. From the figure, we observe that the two cost metrics are monotonically changing and cycle time reaches a saturation point, so that allocating more powerful resources is meaningless. The exact balance between cost and cycle time to be decided depends on the weight of each optimization criterion. The above example is typical to several cases, but there are also several cases where the trade-offs are more complex and the solution space has less intuitive local and global optima, e.g., when the two cost metrics are combined in a non-linear objective function.

Allocating resources to a graph of connected tasks, so that the allocation regarding a specific task impacts on the other tasks, is a problem that has appeared in several flavors in data analytics, e.g., [20,30,35,36], all of them corresponding to NP-hard problems. This implies that formulating the problem in a form, such as ILP, does not scale. Therefore, there are four main options remaining, using the work in [36] as an example of investigating all of them:

1. Heuristics that operate directly on the formal problem formulation, e.g., through restricting the possible allocation solutions to attain scalability.
2. Greedy heuristics.
3. Heuristics that are based on local search methods.
4. Other heuristics, mostly, nature-inspired ones [12].

The works in [20,30,35,36], although they deal with different problem flavors, agree in that there is no *one-size-fits-all*, but in most cases the two main observations are: (i) greedy heuristics are very fast but they miss good trade-off between conflicting objectives; and (ii) local search methods are the most effective in striking good balance between such objectives. More importantly, local search methods are easy to develop and effective, provided that they start exploring the search point quite close to an acceptable final solution.

In summary, a high-level approach to handling the generic BP case can be as follows. We first compute the minimum cost and we define, through a user-defined threshold ϵ, the degradation in the cost that the BP designer can tolerate. Given the cost constraint, we search for the best cycle time. The exact optimality search policy is left for the user: in principle all brute force, greedy and more stochastic solutions apply. In cases where the initial solution, e.g., derived by rules or a polynomial algorithm or through optimizing one objective as above, is adequately satisfactory and it is reasonable to assume that a better solution can be produced through fine-tuning, methodologies that focus on the near neighborhood, such as iterated local search, are preferable. In cases where a vast search space should be covered efficiently, we should also employ methodologies, such as genetic algorithms.

6   Discussion

In this section, we discuss software development and open issues.

6.1   Development Issues

For understanding the trade-offs when modifying the actor properties as discussed in Sect. 5.2, existing tools, such as the BIMP simulator [2], are adequate.

However, automated re-ordering of tasks is a functionality that does not exist in modern tools for free. As a side-product of this manuscript, we have developed a software prototype that extends the Camunda BP management software [4] but can also support other BPM tools.

The software prototype consists of two main parts. The first part is a BPMN parser, which extracts the vertices that represent the tasks of the process, and the edges from the input BPMN file. To this end, we process the XML representation of the process model, which has the following form:

```
...
<bpmn:startEvent id="StartEvent_1">
  <bpmn:outgoing>SequenceFlow_11y212g</bpmn:outgoing>
</bpmn:startEvent>
<bpmn:task id="A" name="Task A">
  <bpmn:incoming>SequenceFlow_11y212g</bpmn:incoming>
  <bpmn:outgoing>SequenceFlow_02dhphd</bpmn:outgoing>
</bpmn:task>
...
<bpmn:endEvent id="EndEvent_1m1wp9j">
  <bpmn:incoming>SequenceFlow_1cm7151</bpmn:incoming>
</bpmn:endEvent>
<bpmn:sequenceFlow id="SequenceFlow_11y212g"
  sourceRef="StartEvent_1" targetRef="A" />
...
```

In the above example, a start event is followed by a task with id A. Essentially, the Camunda parser searches for bpmn:startEvent, bpmn:endEvent, bpmn:task and bpmn:sequenceFlow XML elements.

The second part takes as input the output of the first part and additionally the metadata regarding the corresponding BP, namely, task selectivity, cost of execution and precedence constraints, which are assumed to be known. Finally, the process is optimized according to the algorithm presented and is output as a BPMN XML file, where the bpmn:sequenceFlow, bpmn:incoming and bpmn:outgoing elements are defined according to the optimized process model.

The prototype mentioned above is capable of performing automated optimization, provided that the required metadata exist. Following up on the discussion in Sect. 2, to date, there is not a clear solution to the issue of their automated extraction. In order to solve this issue, we advocate an approach that relies on BP event log analysis and/or declarative process modeling, as in [33,37,38].

A set of BP event log analysis techniques that aim to extract BP metadata have been proposed. For example, in [6], the replay method is presented, where, after the process model extraction from the logs is complete, every event log case is attempted to be "replayed" (i.e. re-executed) using each of the extracted models. As a result, the fitness of each of the extracted models is calculated. Additionally, this method can be used to collect various type of statistics regarding the execution of the process. These include task duration, which is related to execution cost, and routing probabilities (e.g. in OR gateways) which is related to selectivity. Regarding precedence constraints, the focus is shifted towards behavioral relations that exist between tasks [41,48]. In both approaches, a set of relations (i.e. patterns) are extracted from the event logs; these patterns contain the precedence constraints that exist between the tasks of the process. The complete investigation of the issue of automated metadata extraction capitalizing on existing process mining solutions is complementary to this work and is left as a future extension. Finally, the systematic manual specification of the constraints has already been proposed in [37,38]. The drawback is that the burden is shifted to the process designer to specify such constraints.

6.2 Open Issues

In the previous sections, we provided concrete examples of application of optimization techniques initially proposed for data-centric workflows to BPs along with insights into performance benefits. However, there are several open issues in providing end-to-end solutions. We elaborate on these issues below:

- Even the better investigated type of data-centric workflow optimization, namely task re-ordering, requires extensions to cover generic BP scenarios. For example, in the model in Fig. 3, an optimization might move the expensive supervisor check task in parallel with the check for account existence to decrease cycle time. The current state-of-the-art in algorithms for minimizing response time in data analytic workflows do not account for such model structure modifications in an automated manner [28]; therefore further research is required in this direction.
- In data-centric dataflows, the equivalent of a token is a data record and, typically, we are interested in the performance when processing a large number of such records. The main difference to BPs is that all input records are available at the beginning of the workflow execution; by contrast, in BPs, the tokens arrive according to several types of probability distributions. In addition, in data-centric workflows, it is important to measure the time of processing for the whole input dataset, whereas in BPs, the cycle time refers to the time of processing a single input token taking into consideration any waiting times. The cost models in data-centric workflows [29] need to be extended to better cover these aspects, e.g., nowadays they are inadequate to cover all metrics in the BIMP simulator [2].
- In the optimization algorithms presented in Sect. 5.1, we split BP graphs into branches. For developing more holistic solutions, we need further constraint types apart from precedence ones, e.g., to specify that two tasks cannot belong to the same branch. Then, algorithms that can handle such constraints need to be developed.
- The presented solutions rely on the existence of statistical metadata as well; thus extending the current techniques for process monitoring to support metadata extraction is required for rendering the proposed solutions practical as discussed in Sect. 6. Orthogonally, flexibility is a key objective in BPs (see Ch. 8 in [17]); in terms of optimization techniques, flexibility can be manifested

in developing techniques that are robust to small changes in the metadata values. Developing solutions that optimize also for flexibility is an interesting direction for future work that can also benefit from advances in the data management community [53].

– The optimization solutions presented are automated but this does not imply that they can enact automated optimizations in the actual running business processes in an organization. For example, the algorithm may advocate doubling the capacity of a specific resource type. However, they do not specify whether this can be achieved by modifying the duties of personnel, hiring new staff, upgrading some software system and so on.

– The mapping process from BPMN to DAGs in Sect. 4.1 has not been explored thoroughly and validated in arbitrary scenarios. More work is needed in order not only to map BP models to DAGs but also to map the optimized DAG back to a BP model. This needs to be coupled with mechanisms for eligibility assessment of BP models as to whether it is possible and/or meaningful to perform the mapping (see [49] for an early proposal on these issues).

– This methodology can be easily adapted to other process modelling languages and approaches, such as refined process trees [50], where each block can be mapped to a vertex, and Event-driven Process Chains. In the future, we plan to investigate this issue in depth.

7   Conclusions

In this work, we aim to introduce the benefits from transferring big data technologies to business process optimization, in line with the broader vision in [44]. Process mining already plays a significant role in business process management; the key idea behind this work is that, apart from process mining, advanced data management solutions can offer many additional benefits when transferred to business process scenarios. We specifically focus on optimizing aspects such as total cost and cycle time, for which the counterpart techniques in data-centric workflows seem more mature. Data-centric workflows traditionally emphasize on improvements in large flows processing huge amounts of data; however, here we aim to show that they are useful even in small real-life processes as well, yielding improvements up to several times, especially when there are knock-out tasks with flexible ordering. We present complete algorithmic solutions for reordering tasks and systematically exploring the search space of possible solutions under two conflicting objectives, whereas we also describe software implementation aspects of our proposal. For devising end-to-end solutions, we discuss issues remaining open, which range from new algorithms to further work on modeling and process monitoring to collect the necessary metadata.

References

1. Appian: Low-code platform and bpm software for digital transformation. https://www.appian.com/

2. BIMP - the business process simulator. http://bimp.cs.ut.ee/
3. Bizagi - digital transformation and business process management bpm. https://www.bizagi.com/en
4. Camunda bpm: Workflow and decision automation platform. https://camunda.com/
5. van der Aalst, W.M.P.: Re-engineering knock-out processes. Decis. Support Syst. **30**(4), 451–468 (2001)
6. van der Aalst, W.M.P.: Process Mining - Discovery, Conformance and Enhancementof Business Processes. Springer, Heidelberg (2011). https://doi.org/10.1007/978-3-642-19345-3
7. van der Aalst, W.M.P.: Spreadsheets for business process management: using process mining to deal with "events" rather than "numbers"? Bus. Proc. Manag. J. **24**(1), 105–127 (2018)
8. Agrawal, K., Benoit, A., Dufossé, F., Robert, Y.: Mapping filtering streaming applications. Algorithmica **62**(1–2), 258–308 (2012)
9. Augusto, A., Conforti, R., Dumas, M., Rosa, M.L.: Split miner: discovering accurate and simple business process models from event logs. In: 2017 IEEE International Conference on Data Mining, ICDM 2017, New Orleans, LA, USA, 18–21 November 2017, pp. 1–10 (2017)
10. Augusto, A., Conforti, R., Dumas, M., Rosa, M.L., Bruno, G.: Automated discovery of structured process models from event logs: the discover-and-structure approach. Data Knowl. Eng. **117**, 373–392 (2018)
11. Jagadeesh Chandra Bose, R.P., van der Aalst, W.: Trace alignment in process mining: opportunities for process diagnostics. In: Hull, R., Mendling, J., Tai, S. (eds.) BPM 2010. LNCS, vol. 6336, pp. 227–242. Springer, Heidelberg (2010). https://doi.org/10.1007/978-3-642-15618-2_17
12. Brownlee, J.: Clever algorithms: nature-inspired programming recipes (2011)
13. Buijs, J.C.A.M., van Dongen, B.F., van der Aalst, W.M.P.: Discovering and navigating a collection of process models using multiple quality dimensions. In: Business Process Management Workshops - BPM 2013 International Workshops, Beijing, China, 26 August 2013, Revised Papers, pp. 3–14 (2013)
14. Buijs, J.C.A.M., van Dongen, B.F., van der Aalst, W.M.P.: Mining configurable process models from collections of event logs. In: Business Process Management - 11th International Conference, BPM 2013, Beijing, China, 26–30 August 2013, Proceedings, pp. 33–48 (2013)
15. Buzacott, J.A.: Commonalities in reengineered business processes: models and issues. Manag. Sci. **42**(5), 768–782 (1996)
16. Deshpande, A., Hellerstein, L.: Parallel pipelined filter ordering with precedence constraints. ACM Trans. Algorithms **8**(4), 41:1–41:38 (2012)
17. Dumas, M., Rosa, M.L., Mendling, J., Reijers, H.A.: Fundamentals of Business Process Management, 2nd edn. Springer, Heidelberg (2018). https://doi.org/10.1007/978-3-642-33143-5
18. Falk, T., Griesberger, P., Leist, S.: Patterns as an artifact for business process improvement - insights from a case study. In: vom Brocke, J., Hekkala, R., Ram, S., Rossi, M. (eds.) DESRIST 2013. LNCS, vol. 7939, pp. 88–104. Springer, Heidelberg (2013). https://doi.org/10.1007/978-3-642-38827-9_7
19. Gounaris, A.: Towards automated performance optimization of BPMN business processes. In: New Trends in Databases and Information Systems - ADBIS 2016 Short Papers and Workshops, pp. 19–28 (2016)

20. Gounaris, A., Kougka, G., Tous, R., Montes, C.T., Torres, J.: Dynamic configuration of partitioning in spark applications. IEEE Trans. Parallel Distrib. Syst. **28**(7), 1891–1904 (2017)
21. Ibaraki, T., Kameda, T.: On the optimal nesting order for computing N-relational joins. ACM Trans. Database Syst. **9**(3), 482–502 (1984)
22. Indulska, M., zur Muehlen, M., Recker, J.: Measuring method complexity: the case of the business process modeling notation. Technical report, BPM Center Report BPM-09-03 (2009). BPMcenter.org
23. Jennings, N.R., Norman, T.J., Faratin, P., O'Brien, P., Odgers, B.: Autonomous agents for business process management. Appl. Artif. Intell. **14**(2), 145–189 (2000)
24. Kiepuszewski, B., ter Hofstede, A.H.M., Bussler, C.J.: On structured workflow modelling. In: Wangler, B., Bergman, L. (eds.) CAiSE 2000. LNCS, vol. 1789, pp. 431–445. Springer, Heidelberg (2000). https://doi.org/10.1007/3-540-45140-4_29
25. Köpke, J., Franceschetti, M., Eder, J.: Optimizing data-flow implementations for inter-organizational processes. Distrib. Parallel Databases **37**, 651–695 (2018)
26. Kougka, G., Gounaris, A.: Cost optimization of data flows based on task re-ordering. In: Hameurlain, A., Küng, J., Wagner, R., Akbarinia, R., Pacitti, E. (eds.) Transactions on Large-Scale Data- and Knowledge-Centered Systems XXXIII. LNCS, vol. 10430, pp. 113–145. Springer, Heidelberg (2017). https://doi.org/10.1007/978-3-662-55696-2_4
27. Kougka, G., Gounaris, A.: Optimal task ordering in chain data flows: exploring the practicality of non-scalable solutions. In: Bellatreche, L., Chakravarthy, S. (eds.) DaWaK 2017. LNCS, vol. 10440, pp. 19–32. Springer, Cham (2017). https://doi.org/10.1007/978-3-319-64283-3_2
28. Kougka, G., Gounaris, A.: Optimization of data flow execution in a parallel environment. Distrib. Parallel Databases (2018). https://doi.org/10.1007/s10619-018-7243-3
29. Kougka, G., Gounaris, A., Simitsis, A.: The many faces of data-centric workflow optimization: a survey. Int. J. Data Sci. Anal. **6**(2), 81–107 (2018)
30. Kougka, G., Gounaris, A., Tsichlas, K.: Practical algorithms for execution engine selection in data flows. Future Generation Comp. Syst. **45**, 133–148 (2015)
31. Krishnamurthy, R., Boral, H., Zaniolo, C.: Optimization of nonrecursive queries. In: VLDB, pp. 128–137 (1986)
32. La Rosa, M., Dumas, M., ter Hofstede, A.H.M., Mendling, J.: Configurable multi-perspective business process models. Inf. Syst. **36**(2), 313–340 (2011)
33. Maggi, F.M., Mooij, A.J., van der Aalst, W.M.P.: User-guided discovery of declarative process models. In: Proceedings of the IEEE Symposium on Computational Intelligence and Data Mining, CIDM 2011, part of the IEEE Symposium Series on Computational Intelligence 2011, Paris, France, 11–15 April 2011, pp. 192–199 (2011)
34. Mendling, J.: Metrics for Process Models: Empirical Foundations of Verification, Error Prediction, and Guidelines for Correctness. Lecture Notes in Business Information Processing, vol. 6. Springer, Heidelberg (2008). https://doi.org/10.1007/978-3-540-89224-3
35. Michailidou, A., Gounaris, A.: Bi-objective traffic optimization in geo-distributed data flows. Big Data Res. **16**, 36–48 (2019)
36. Nardelli, M., Cardellini, V., Grassi, V., Presti, F.L.: Efficient operator placement for distributed data stream processing applications. IEEE Trans. Parallel Distrib. Syst. **30**(8), 1753–1767 (2019)

37. Pesic, M., van der Aalst, W.M.P.: A declarative approach for flexible business processes management. In: Eder, J., Dustdar, S. (eds.) BPM 2006. LNCS, vol. 4103, pp. 169–180. Springer, Heidelberg (2006). https://doi.org/10.1007/11837862_18
38. Pesic, M., Schonenberg, H., van der Aalst, W.M.P.: DECLARE: full support for loosely-structured processes. In: 11th IEEE International Enterprise Distributed Object Computing Conference (EDOC 2007), pp. 287–300 (2007)
39. Polyvyanyy, A., García-Bañuelos, L., Dumas, M.: Structuring acyclic process models. Inf. Syst. **37**(6), 518–538 (2012)
40. Polyvyanyy, A., Ouyang, C., Barros, A., van der Aalst, W.M.P.: Process querying: enabling business intelligence through query-based process analytics. Decis. Support Syst. **100**, 41–56 (2017)
41. Pourmasoumi, A., Bagheri, E.: Business process mining. CoRR abs/1607.00607 (2016)
42. Rheinländer, A., Leser, U., Graefe, G.: Optimization of complex dataflows with user-defined functions. ACM Comput. Surv. **50**(3), 38:1–38:39 (2017)
43. Rosa, M.L., et al.: Managing process model complexity via abstract syntax modifications. IEEE Trans. Ind. Inf. **7**(4), 614–629 (2011)
44. Sakr, S., Maamar, Z., Awad, A., Benatallah, B., van der Aalst, W.M.P.: Business process analytics and big data systems: a roadmap to bridge the gap. IEEE Access **6**, 77308–77320 (2018)
45. Schunselaar, D.: Configurable process trees: elicitation, analysis, and enactment (2016)
46. Simitsis, A., Wilkinson, K., Castellanos, M., Dayal, U.: Optimizing analytic data flows for multiple execution engines. In: SIGMOD Conference, pp. 829–840 (2012)
47. Simitsis, A., Wilkinson, K., Dayal, U., Castellanos, M.: Optimizing ETL workflows for fault-tolerance. In: ICDE, pp. 385–396 (2010)
48. Tao, J., Deokar, A.V.: An organizational mining approach based on behavioral process patterns. In: 20th Americas Conference on Information Systems, AMCIS 2014, Savannah, Georgia, USA, 7–9 August 2014 (2014)
49. Tsakalidis, G., Vergidis, K., Kougka, G., Gounaris, A.: Eligibility of BPMN models for business process redesign. Information **10**(7), 225 (2019)
50. Vanhatalo, J., Völzer, H., Koehler, J.: The refined process structure tree. In: Dumas, M., Reichert, M., Shan, M.-C. (eds.) BPM 2008. LNCS, vol. 5240, pp. 100–115. Springer, Heidelberg (2008). https://doi.org/10.1007/978-3-540-85758-7_10
51. Varol, Y.L., Rotem, D.: An algorithm to generate all topological sorting arrangements. Comput. J. **24**(1), 83–84 (1981)
52. Vergidis, K., Tiwari, A., Majeed, B.: Business process analysis and optimization: beyond reengineering. IEEE Trans. Syst. Man Cybern. Part C (Appl. Rev.) **38**(1), 69–82 (2008)
53. Wolf, F., Brendle, M., May, N., Willems, P.R., Sattler, K., Grossniklaus, M.: Robustness metrics for relational query execution plans. PVLDB **11**(11), 1360–1372 (2018)
54. Yilmaz, O., Karagoz, P.: Generating performance improvement suggestions by using cross-organizational process mining. In: Proceedings of the 5th International Symposium on Data-driven Process Discovery and Analysis (SIMPDA 2015), Vienna, Austria, 9–11 December 2015, pp. 3–17 (2015)

55. Zaharia, M., et al.: Apache spark: a unified engine for big data processing. Commun. ACM **59**(11), 56–65 (2016)
56. van Zelst, S.J., van Dongen, B.F., van der Aalst, W.M.P.: Event stream-based process discovery using abstract representations. Knowl. Inf. Syst. **54**(2), 407–435 (2018)

A New Knowledge Capitalization Framework in the Big Data Context Through Shared Parameters Experiences

Badr Hirchoua[1](✉), Brahim Ouhbi[1], Bouchra Frikh[2], and Ismail Khalil[3]

[1] National Higher School of Arts and Crafts (ENSAM), Industrial Engineering and Productivity Department, Moulay Ismail University (UMI), Meknes, Morocco
Badr.hirchoua@gmail.com, ouhbib@yahoo.co.uk
[2] Higher School of Technology (EST), Computer Science Department, Sidi Mohamed Ben Abdellah University (USMBA), Fez, Morocco
bfrikh@yahoo.com
[3] Institute Telecooperation, Johannes Kepler University, Linz, Austria
Ismail.khalil@jku.at

Abstract. Knowledge management proves to be inexorable in generating value from disorganized knowledge bases, as well as separating concerns through intelligent knowledge capitalization system in the big data context. Such systems, however, require a long and challenging learning process and complex parameters tuning in order to push the capitalization process forward.

In this paper, a new knowledge capitalization framework is introduced as an adaptive and intelligent technique, acting on top of a distributed system and running on a large scale. This framework is a three-level paradigm in which each knowledge base is modeled as a mixture over an underlying set of knowledge groups. Each group is, in turn, formed as a mixture over a latent set of knowledge entities. Besides, focusing on each model separately and tuning its parameters require more extended time and resources to find the optimal configuration, so the proposed approach uses the shared parameter mechanism driven by the group coherence metric. It relies on this paradigm to increase the model's quality, improve knowledge entities' coherence, and advance the groups' smoothness and density. Results reveal significant and robust consistency amongst different knowledge groups. Additionally, each distributed model is updated three times on average. A straightforward adaptation of each model can lead to an improved model, with an augmentation of 20% in the group coherence. Finally, a knowledge retrieval system is developed to verify the appropriateness and efficacy of the formed groups as well as to evaluate the response time and precision.

Keywords: Knowledge capitalization · Data intelligence · Knowledge management · Big data computing · Shared parameters

© Springer-Verlag GmbH Germany, part of Springer Nature 2020
A. Hameurlain and A Min Tjoa (Eds.): TLDKS XLIII, LNCS 12130, pp. 86–113, 2020.
https://doi.org/10.1007/978-3-662-62199-8_4

1   Introduction

The definition of knowledge has been a debate amongst academics across disciplines for many years [18]. Many researchers during the last years have addressed the theory of knowledge management (KM). Notwithstanding, several studies have distinguished four steps of the KM process: creation, storage, distribution, and use of knowledge to enhance the impact of knowledge on critical goals achievement [18,21]. However, determining knowledge requirements and obtaining pertinent, consistent, and up-to-date knowledge is a complex process. The process of KM is going to take all its senses when knowledge is reused [14]. In other words, when it provides relevant knowledge to assist users/systems in executing knowledge-intensive tasks at the right time and in the proper form [9].

In recent years, businesses are expecting significant data growth in terms of volume, velocity, and variety. In practice, traditional architectures are grossly insufficient and cannot adequately analyze the big data, which contains valuable knowledge [19,23,29,50]. Given the distinct prosperous opportunities provided by KM in the big data, it is still not exploited successfully due to different causes. The reasons can be the lack of necessary knowledge or the absence of essential knowledge resources, but more important yet, the organized knowledge cannot be easily obtained and understood [4,8,16]. These reasons can be deemed interrelated in such context.

Knowledge capitalization is an essential part of the knowledge creation process. Knowledge capitalization refers to the process through which knowledge is adapted, adopted by other systems, and up-scaled, leading to a more significant impact in future knowledge uses by improving the knowledge quality [3]. The knowledge capitalization framework must take the advantages of the learning effect and prevent the system from falling into poor knowledge practices [43], especially in the big data context. Traditional knowledge capitalization approaches are facing the problem of reinventing past solutions, instead of exploiting the previous accumulated experiences. Consequently, the general process produces a knowledge loss, increases the dependency on some expertise, but more important yet, it makes the evolution of the accumulated knowledge more difficult.

Nevertheless, integrative studies that combine big data analytics and KM are scarce, which produces a gap in the literature concerning the topic. Companies have been gathering and capitalizing on data for years [28]. However, the newly captured data is entirely different regarding volume, velocity, and variety, and thus it demands exceptional methods, tools, and technologies to be adopted [16]. Therefore, the stored knowledge needs to be analyzed comprehensively to conduct a practical knowledge capitalization approach with the cumulative experience.

However, various extensions have emerged to cope with knowledge capitalization problems in big data context. The primary problem noted by Becerra et al. [5] is how to set a link between big data and knowledge? Many researchers, including Yang et al. [52], worked on the literature concerning KM to develop a big data vision that fits with existing theories, such as the difficulties of transforming the enormous quantity of non-structured data into a general knowledge [44], or to structured information [30]. Lopez et al. [31] created a knowledge-based maintenance approach framework, which aimed to preserve the valuable experiences and knowledge. In the same context, Fan et al. [15] used the stored information from past experiences to present a temporal knowledge discovery method. Furthermore, Ruiz et al. [42] proposed a framework that manages and generates knowledge from information on experiences. Their framework suggested a fundamental experience feedback process dedicated to maintenance, allowing the capitalization on past activities. Even though these KM systems extensions have reached a certain level of success, their direct application to the big data is still limited due to the particular challenges discussed above.

In this paper, we are interested in handling three significant challenges related to big data context to push the capitalization process forward. Firstly, the duplication detection from large knowledge datasets (Volume), where KM systems face a diversity of datasets from different sources and domains. These datasets consist of multiple modalities, each of which has a diverse representation, distribution, scale, and density. Usually, the need is to harness multiple disparate datasets [47]. Secondly, the semantic relations between different knowledge entities must be preserved (Variety), where each knowledge-base contains semantic relationships between knowledge entities. Therefore, keeping these relations while merging different knowledge bases is challenging. Finally, the time response for a given request/query refers to time-critical systems [2] (Velocity). Indeed, these systems present temporal restrictions, which typically consist of maximum deadlines for requests to be processed and the output to be generated. Typical time-critical systems [57] have benefited from different general-purpose computational infrastructures that take advantage of the application characterization to estimate a priori the maximum response times. In this sense, let us take the biomedical domain as an example to understand those limitations considering the access time. Traditional methods consume $12\,\mathrm{s}$ on average in the reusing phase [12], whereas in big data context, our experiments show that the reusing time is $0.061\,\mathrm{s}$ on average.

Due to the described limitations of existing methods, and motivated by different challenges discussed above, we propose a novel common control knowledge capitalization system concerned with designing strategies operating in a distributed environment. The proposal aims to achieve a global control objective through this environment. However, the primary goal in the knowledge capitalization system is to gain value from the big knowledge bases. Besides, making sense of large amounts of disorganized knowledge has always been the defining challenge of KM. This paper simplifies this problem by grouping coherent knowledge entities from different sources into the same group. This approach allows the identification of coherent knowledge groups, guarantees the response precision, and ensures the fast and accurate access to the capitalized knowledge. It is a three-level paradigm, in which each knowledge base is modeled as a mixture over a hidden set of knowledge groups. Each group is distributed according to a probability distribution of the knowledge entities. For a given knowledge base, the system starts by identifying the distribution of knowledge entities. Then, it groups these entities according to their similarity in a distributed environment. Therefore, each distributed site contains only the correlated knowledge.

Given a learning algorithm capable of handling big knowledge bases, we still need to ensure the fastest convergence. Even with simple restrictions, there are hundreds of possible configurations, parameters, and conflict situations—many of which yield potent combinations. It is not easy to explore this combinatorially-vast configurations space efficiently. The developed system learns from self-configuring (starting from basic settings), which provides a cumulated experience for building accurate distributed models. In order to ensure the convergence of different models with optimal training time, the proposed framework identifies the most robust parameter combination and share it across different sites. In each distributed site, the first model uses a self-estimated parameter sequence. Then, with further model training, the parameters configuration become proficient at identifying high-level settings, which are estimated using the group coherence metrics. This additional feature is necessary for the system performances. It controls the entire system configurations rather than focusing on each model separately, which will necessitate a considerable time and resources. Therefore, it makes the constructed knowledge groups more coherent in terms of knowledge entities it contains. It ensures the high accuracy in the trained models by tuning different parameters using the past models' experiences. The proposed system is evaluated through an experimental study using different real-world knowledge bases and various metrics. Results reveal significant and robust consistency amongst different knowledge groups. Additionally, each distributed model is rebuilt three times on average. A straightforward update of each model can lead to an upgraded model, with an increase of 20% in the group coherence. Finally, the developed knowledge retrieval system confirms the appropriateness and efficacy of the formed groups as well as it demonstrates the response time and precision performances. Overall, this paper makes the following contributions:

1. It proposes a new knowledge capitalization framework for jointly learning the knowledge group distributions.
2. It captures the correlation between knowledge entities and demonstrates that the model accuracy can be improved via the new shared parameters mechanism.
3. It extends the learning process and preserves higher-order semantics patterns between knowledge entities efficiently.
4. It can enhance semantic relations between knowledge entities, whether or not they appear in the same knowledge base.
5. It handles the big data issues, by proposing a distributed learning process.

The remainder of this paper is organized as follows: Sect. 2 discusses some of the related research efforts and highlights them. Section 3 describes the proposed approach and provides an illustrative example of the proposed method. Section 4 is devoted to the experimental settings, measures and methodology, and experimental results. Conclusions and proposals for future work are summarized in Sect. 5.

2   Related Works

This section includes and briefly describes some of the research works that have addressed the same problems handled in this work. Accurately, the general idea and some shortcomings for these methods will be presented, if any. Also, these methods involved in many assumptions, so they will have a brief idea of what hypothesis these methods can improve with.

Traditionally, KM systems are utilized to identify, share, and capitalize on the knowledge. Additionally, they are applied to organize knowledge into processes. As big data is transforming the nature of data altogether, the volume, velocity, and variety of information is immense. Therefore, the KM becomes more challenging. Many previous researches have focused on distinguishing influencing factors of successful KM [5,15,31,42,44,52]. Teresa et al. [45] defined KM capability as the ability to acquire, convert, and apply knowledge. Meanwhile, Wang et al. [48] revealed that knowledge sharing is an action where system components can interchange expertise and contribute to the application of knowledge. Additionally, Gao et al. [18] considered knowledge application as an ability to discover, recognize, and employ the stored knowledge. In contrast, knowledge application intends to develop new knowledge through integration, innovation, and enlargement of existing knowledge base [33]. In the context of big data, the new and novel extracted knowledge, through innovative and advanced analytics tools, will extend the existing knowledge base.

Ouided et al. [36] used the Return of EXperience (REX) method to capitalize on the knowledge corporate. Contrary to the proposed approach, which capitalizes the knowledge without referring to any external signal, the REX method capitalized on strategic knowledge and favoured experience feedback. This process indicates a need to understand the various perceptions of the capitalization process, that exist among stored experiences. Moreover, Zhang et al. [55,56] proposed a case-based reasoning (CBR) experiences capitalization system. The CBR used the stored knowledge, captured new knowledge, and made it immediately available for solving the next problems. However, there has been little discussion about the usefulness of the knowledge capitalization in different industries, especially the impact of reducing human effort and time. In this field, Rodriguez et al. [41] tackled this problem in the automotive industry, which attempted to introduce new employees to their respective roles and duties in a faster way. The critical research question handled by Rasovska et al. [39] was the use of a mixed-method of knowledge capitalization in maintenance. This method integrated a representation and a reasoning model, both completing each other to represent and manipulate the domain knowledge known as capitalization.

Oramas et al. [35] presented and evaluated an information extraction pipeline for a music knowledge base construction. The semantic relations between similar entities are grouped into clusters by exploiting syntactic dependencies. Next, these relations are ranked using a new confidence measure based on statistical and linguistic evidence. This method demonstrated to discover new facts with high precision, which are missed in the current generic, as well as in the music-specific knowledge repositories. Therefore, the proposed work makes a significant contribution to research on knowledge capitalization by discovering new knowledge, as well as restructuring it to be reused by different users/systems. Zwicklbauer et al. [58] proposed a framework, which initially generated a semantic embedding entity automatically. Then, the system collectively linked the input to an entity in a knowledge base with a graph-based approach.

Paredes et al. [37] presented a new method for rule extraction in knowledge-based systems. This method consisted of retrieving an initial set of rules extracted from a knowledge base, used conventional logical approaches, and then ranked this initial set of rules by applying a multicriteria decision analysis method. Their method can be used to implement a knowledge-based management system, which can be a preparation step for the knowledge capitalization system. The knowledge capitalization depends on the context in which would be applied; hence, Esposito et al. [13] discussed the same problem and proposed an alternative solution to overtake two fundamental issues: data heterogeneity and advanced processing capabilities. They have presented a knowledge-based solution for big data analytics, which consisted of applying automatic schema mapping to face data heterogeneity issues. Moreover, they designed and implemented a flexible architectural platform providing distributed mining solutions for vast amounts of unstructured data. The proposed system findings make an essential contribution to the field of knowledge-based solutions for big data by surpassing the knowledge-based enforcement to publish/subscribe services.

The knowledge capitalization attempts to favour the growth, transmission, and conservation of knowledge in the organization, with the view of preserving and sharing. The corporate memories construction has become a necessity in current practice [27]. Table 1 shows a comparative study using different metrics, by which the proposed approach is compared to the similar works. The distributed mechanism is one of the big data evolution axes, especially with the growth of knowledge base size. The knowledge update and scalability metrics are reported to illustrate the challenges of the durability of the developed systems in response to the knowledge streaming issue [46]. The multi-domain application reveals in addition to the semantic metric, the strength of the proposed approach, mainly by keeping the semantic relationships even in different domains, and enhance semantic relations between knowledge entities, whether or not they appear in the same knowledge base. Finally, the knowledge capitalization is examined by a knowledge retrieval system to inspect the intelligent use of capitalized knowledge.

In our previous works, [26, 27], we found that the latent Dirichlet allocation (LDA) [6] is helpful for knowledge capitalization in the big data context. This paper extends our previous conference article [26] with the following improvements. 1) We introduce the shared parameters mechanism to improve the model and knowledge group quality, where the groups' coherence is highly verified. 2)

Table 1. Comparative study.

	Big data context	Distributed system	Knowledge update	Multi domain	Knowledge retrieval	Semantic	Scalability
The proposed system	✓	✓	✓	✓	✓	✓	✓
Gangemi et al. [17]	-	-	-	✓	-	✓	-
Hellmann et al. [25]	-	✓	✓	✓	✓	✓	✓
Oramas et al. [35]	✓	-	✓	✓	✓	✓	-
Ouided et al. [36]	-	-	-	✓	-	-	-
Perner et al. [38]	-	-	-	-	✓	✓	-
Ruiz et al. [42]	-	-	-	✓	✓	✓	-
Yang et al. [51]	-	✓	-	✓	✓	✓	✓
Zenkert et al. [54]	✓	-	-	✓	✓	✓	-

The capability of knowledge capitalization and knowledge discovery is demonstrated. 3) More comprehensive experiments were conducted, and new findings are reported.

In this paper, a novel shared parameter approach in the big data context is proposed. To the best of the authors' knowledge, there is no work addressed the issues mentioned above as of yet. Therefore, making knowledge groups coherence is the main contribution of this paper. The proposed approach integrates the shared parameters paradigm to compare the distributed model accuracy, that permits solving complex knowledge capitalization problems. This paper illustrates the proposed solution in the big data context that connects users/systems to the exact knowledge they need at the time they need it – when they are performing a task, making a decision, or solving a problem as quickly as possible.

In Sect. 3, the novel knowledge capitalization approach is described, and an illustrative example is included.

3   Knowledge Capitalization

In this section, the novel knowledge capitalization approach is proposed, and the shared parameter mechanism is detailed. Moreover, an illustrative example is provided to demonstrate the strength and efficiency of the proposed framework.

3.1   Knowledge Capitalization Framework

In the big data context, the advanced KM systems can increase the knowledge value by providing immediate performance feedback. These systems have steadily and progressively improved knowledge quality. Traditional KM systems mainly assume that the input has a unique schema and rigid semantics. Besides, the volumes and heterogeneity of the input sources increase several inconsistencies, which make the big data an intensive area of experience. Specifically, knowledge in the big data era is dynamic, grows with technology, and with different practices. Besides, the changes related to new techniques, technologies, and methodologies are constant. Therefore, the knowledge and experience collected overhead the times play a crucial role. Knowledge capitalization allows the knowledge produced during the diverse processes to be organized and reused, which thus improves its quality and productivity.

The proposed framework aims at maximizing knowledge quality and contributes to building actionable distributed knowledge groups. It starts by capturing the knowledge entities encoded in a knowledge base and then creating coherent knowledge groups that are shared across the environment. Analogically to the latent Dirichlet allocation topic modelling [6], where every document is modelled as a mixture of latent topics, and every topic is represented as the distribution of words; a knowledge base exhibits a mixture of latent groups' representation, which in turn consists of the knowledge entities distribution characterizes each group. A knowledge-base is a special kind of database for KM. In other words, a knowledge base is an information repository that provides a means for information to be collected, organized, shared, and searched. It represents facts about the world, often in the form of ontology. Recently, ontologies have boomed as an essential component to represent different knowledge domains. The ontology encompasses a representation of concepts and relations between entities that substantiate one, many, or all domains of discourse. In this paper, we assume that the ontologies are represented using the Web Ontology Language (OWL) [22], which is a Semantic Web language designed to represent rich and sophisticated knowledge.

Notation: let B be the number of the knowledge bases, G the number of groups, k represents the number of knowledge entities over knowledge bases, and k_b is the number of knowledge entities in the knowledge base b. $\vec{\phi}_g$ is a k dimensional categorical distribution over knowledge entities, with symmetric Dirichlet prior β. $\vec{\theta}_b$ is the proportion for knowledge base b with Dirichlet prior α. (Z_{b_i}, E_{b_i}) is the assignment and knowledge entity respectively on position i of the knowledge base b. The matrix $\theta = (\vec{\theta}_1, \ldots, \vec{\theta}_B)$ is formed by all groups proportions.

Generally, knowledge groups are produced using the following process:

– Predict the number N of knowledge entities which the group will contain (according to the Poisson distribution).
– Choose a group mixture for the knowledge base (according to a Dirichlet distribution over a fixed set of G groups).
– Generate each knowledge entity $E_{(i)}$ in the knowledge base by:
  • Picking a group (according to the multinomial distribution that was sampled above).
  • Using the group to generate the knowledge entity itself (according to the group's multinomial distribution).

Formally, Algorithm 1 ensures the generative process, and Fig. 1 explains the interaction between the models' parameters and the knowledge base production.

Algorithm 1. The model's generative process in each distributed site.

1: **for** $b \in \{1, \ldots, B\}$ **do**
2:     Predict $N \sim$ Poisson (ξ).
3:     Choose $\vec{\theta}_b \sim Dir(\alpha)$.
4:     **for** $i \in \{1, \ldots, k_b\}$ **do**
5:         Choose a group $Z_{b_i} \sim Mult(\vec{\theta}_b)$.
6:         Choose a knowledge entity $E_{b_i} \sim Dir(\vec{\phi}_{Z_{b_i}})$ from $p(E_{(n)} / Z_{b_n}, \beta)$, the
            multinomial probability conditioned on group Z_{b_n}.
7:     **end for**
8: **end for**

The Dirichlet is a convenient distribution, which has the following properties: it is in the exponential family, has finite-dimensional sufficient statistics, and is conjugate to the multinomial distribution. The k-dimensional Dirichlet random variable θ can take values in the $(k-1)$ simplex (a k-vector θ lies in the $(k-1)$ simplex if $\theta_i \geq 0, \sum_{i=1}^k \theta_i = 1$), and has the following probability density on this simplex:

$$p(\theta|\alpha) = \frac{\Gamma(\sum_{i=1}^k \alpha_i)}{\prod_{i=1}^k \Gamma(\alpha_i)} \theta_1^{\alpha_1 - 1} \ldots \theta_k^{\alpha_k - 1}, \tag{1}$$

where the parameter α is a k-vector with components $\alpha_i > 0$, and $\Gamma(x)$ is the Gamma function.

One KM milestone in the big data context is to exceed knowledge capabilities in a complex environment. Relative to previous KM pillars, the proposed framework is trained to maximize the knowledge group coherence and to improve the knowledge quality. Thus, it guarantees this process by using a distributed training method based on a novel massively-scaled version of parameter sharing driven by knowledge group coherence. Specifically, the distributed training process is separated into four components, as illustrated in Fig. 2. Each distributed site contains a single agent that can access the local knowledge base, build the local model, and emits the model performances as well as the parameters configuration. It worth mentioning that the local models are constructed and modelled independently. The optimizer concerned by performing the parameter refinement via the group coherence metric. This process is achieved by utilizing the gathered and centralized experiences from distributed models in terms of parameters set, as well as the group coherence metric. The local agents synchronize their experience through refreshing their local parameters, where each agent evaluates the trained models using the refined parameters set. During synchronous model construction, each agent updates its local copy of parameters using the latest configuration. The evaluation agents are charged with merging the resulted models to optimize the access time to the requested knowledge. Notwithstanding, the framework does not contain an explicit communication channel between the distributed sites; the optimizer controls the teamwork. This additional feature restricts the system from dropping into an overtraining issue.

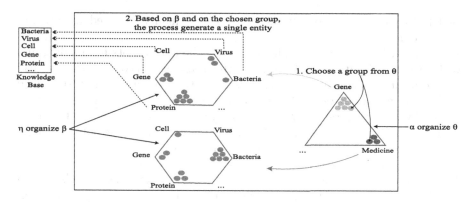

Fig. 1. How a knowledge base is generated. First α organize the θ and then pick a group from θ. Based on the picked group, β is generated. β is organized by η. Finally an entity is picked from β and is putted into the knowledge base.

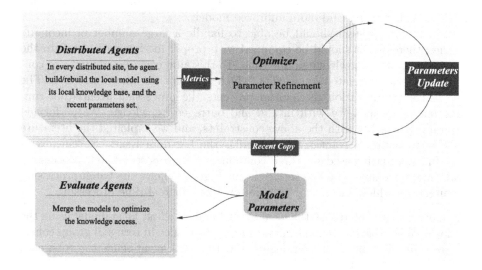

Fig. 2. Basic distributed architecture for the shared parameters approach.

The shared parameters mechanism paradigm has two major decoupled threads; it uses the remote agents in each distributed site, and the recent parameters set collected from past experiences. In the first thread, the agent interacts with the local knowledge bases and guarantees the parameter sequences for the model, which immediately calculates the group coherence values. In the second thread, the agent collects the parameter experiences from different sites. In order to satisfy this behaviour, the parameters update should not move too far from the range of parameters that works for the majority of models with high performances (high coherence values). Notice that in this case, each agent has to refresh its local copy of parameters, to make sure that it is always running with the latest configuration, to keep the local models' quality balanced according to the other sites.

The shared parameters paradigm prevents the local agents from falling into weak repetitive situations, by focusing on the whole system configuration instead of concentrating on each model separately. At the beginning, the first trained local model has less group coherence comparing to the late versions. To force exploration in configuration space, during training (and only during training), we randomized the system's properties. Later on, we identify the optimal configurations when a new model is consistently improving the coherence inside each group. Therefore, gaining the long-term model performances often requires sacrificing the short-term model, since parametrizing such complex models takes a considerable time. This observation reinforces our belief that the system is genuinely optimizing over the short run, considering the big data context. The proposed framework makes it possible to train models capable of achieving sophisticated goals in complex and distributed environments. Parameter sharing mechanism helps algorithms explore their parameter space more effectively, which leads to higher scores and more improved models.

Finally, our system should be able to handle a large number of incoming queries; therefore, it should be equipped with proper mechanisms to return the precise requested knowledge in due time. To this aim, each distributed site contains only the correlated knowledge, which restricts the knowledge loss. The knowledge capitalization mechanism prevents the processing agent from running out of its memory with invalid and outraged knowledge. We performed several experiments with the above constraints, and we exploited the literature on KM to obtain a solution that handles the big data issues. Specifically, a new full approach based on three components is proposed: batch processing, real-time processing, and the service layer. Figure 3 shows the batch processing architecture, which serves as a preparation stage for real-time processing:

1. In every distributed site, the local agent builds the first local model using the local knowledge bases and evaluates its performance in terms of group coherence. In addition to the parameters set, the local agent sends the coherence metrics to the optimizer.
2. The optimizer receives all local copies of parameters from distributed agents and refines them to construct the appropriate copy of parameters. In other words, the optimizer chooses the set of parameters that forms the highest coherent groups for the majority of models.
3. Every distributed agent refreshes its local set of parameters using the latest copy received from the model parameters set.
4. In every distributed site, the agent rebuilds the local model using the latest parameters.
5. The evaluation agents gather all local models from different sites and reorganize the groups over the available site. In other words, the evaluation agents store the correlated groups on the same site, which makes the knowledge access more accurate and fast.

In addition to the Dirichlet distribution advantages discussed above, it also facilitates the development of inference and parameter estimation algorithms.

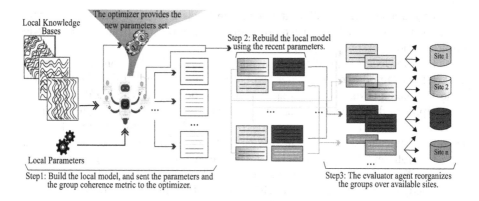

Fig. 3. The batch processing framework.

The inference tries to determine the latent variables that describe the model. Precisely, this step reveals the latent variables collection, which describes the transformation from knowledge groups to allocations, then to assignments. However, changing a group assignment for each entity, given the rest of the entities' assignments, will describe the knowledge base completely except for the particulate entity at each step. The knowledge inference presents an intractability problem. Therefore, given a set of knowledge bases, inferring the exact posterior distribution $P(\theta, \phi, Z/E)$ is intractable. In other words, the normalization factor in particular $P(\theta, \phi, Z/E, \alpha, \beta)$ presented in Eq. 2 cannot be computed exactly.

$$P(\theta, \phi, Z/E, \alpha, \beta) = \frac{P(\theta, \phi, Z, E/\alpha, \beta)}{P(E/\alpha, \beta)} \quad (2)$$

The approximation inference techniques can be applied to handle this issue, where the collapsed Gibbs sampler [20] can guarantee the convergence, but it still weak in knowing how many iterations are required to reach the stationary distribution. However, with the proposed shared parameters mechanism, we were able to form a model that optimizes and simultaneously assures the parameters sequence quality. Besides, the group size value N is independent of all other samples generating variables (θ and Z). This restriction secures the application of the refined parameter sequences to different models, instead of similar models with similar properties.

Given the parameters α and β, the joint distribution of a group mixture θ, a set of groups Z, and a set of N entities E is:

$$p(\theta, Z, E/\alpha, \beta) = p(\theta/\alpha) \prod_{n=1}^{N} p(Z_n/\theta) p(E_n/Z_n, \beta), \quad (3)$$

The marginal distribution of a knowledge base is given by:

$$p(E/\alpha, \beta) = \int p(\theta/\alpha) \left(\prod_{n=1}^{N} \sum_{Z_n} p(Z_n/\theta) p(E_n/Z_n, \beta) \right) d\theta \quad (4)$$

The modelization of different knowledge levels trains a model, which determines better groups that are more human interpretable from the knowledge capitalization perspective [11].

The knowledge capitalization is an objective, where a company wants to make the accumulated knowledge explicitly available and usable; however, this objective has a severe effect on such system, especially in the big data context. The capitalized knowledge accuracy and robustness is tested using a knowledge retrieval service. This service responds to the users' queries by returning the most correlated knowledge entities in due time. Since each distributed site contains only the coherent knowledge entities, the batch processing step guarantees the response precision with the minimum time. The created knowledge groups give a detailed, complete, and global vision about the involved parameters, which provides accurate knowledge entities to the final users.

3.2   Illustration of the Proposed Approach

In this paper, we consider the problem of constructing the high coherence knowledge groups that enable efficient formulation from large knowledge bases while preserving the essential relationships between different entities. The proposed framework is based on a simple exchangeability assumption for the entities and groups in a knowledge base; it is therefore identified by a straightforward application of the shared parameters sequence. The basic idea is that knowledge bases are represented as random mixtures over latent groups, where a distribution over knowledge entities characterizes each group.

It is important to note that the knowledge bases used in this work are represented as ontologies. Therefore, the first step consists of breaking down the input ontology into triplets without losing the semantic relations between entities. Formally, the knowledge nodes are entities and edges are subject-property-object triple facts. Each edge indicates a relationship from entity E_i to entity E_j. In order to quantify the nodes property to be preserved, Fig. 4 represents the adopted transformation process, by which every relationship between two entities is captured.

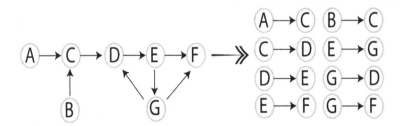

Fig. 4. Knowledge base transformation - identify the possible connections for a given input.

Given a knowledge base (Fig. 5), the proposed framework backtracks and tries to figure out what groups would create this knowledge base in the first place (Fig. 1). In vector space, any knowledge-base can be represented as a KB-KE matrix. Table 2 shows an example of three knowledge bases from Fig. 5 and four knowledge entities "Binding - Cytoplasm - Nucleus - P65". The value of (i, j) cell gives the frequency count of entity E_j in knowledge base b_i.

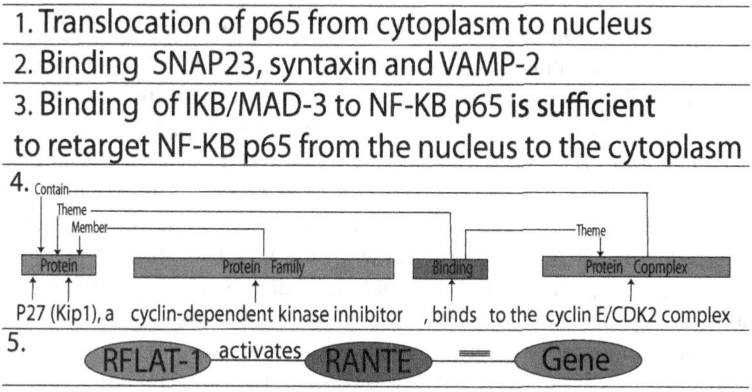

Fig. 5. Example of knowledge bases form.

Table 2. Example of a KB-KE matrix from Fig. 5.

	Binding	Cytoplasm	Nucleus	P65
Knowledge base 1	0	1	1	1
Knowledge base 2	1	0	0	0
Knowledge base 3	1	1	1	2

The proposed system converts the matrix shown in Table 2 into two lower dimensional matrices. The first matrix is a KB-groups matrix shown in Table 3, and the second is a group – entities matrix shown in Table 5, with dimensions (B, G) and (G, K) respectively.

Table 3. Example of a KB-group matrix according to Fig. 5 and Table 2.

	$Z_1 = Binding$	$Z_2 = CellComp$	$Z_3 = Protein$
Knowledge base 1	0.3	0.74	0.6
Knowledge base 2	0.6	0.2	0.83
Knowledge base 3	0.6	0.75	0.89

Table 4. Example of a group-KE matrix according to Fig. 5, Table 2, and Table 3.

	Binding	Cytoplasm	Nucleus	P65
$Z_1 = Binding$	**0.91**	0.05	0.1	0.8
$Z_2 = CellComp$	0.09	**0.93**	**0.94**	0.7
$Z_3 = Protein$	0.5	0.2	0.3	**0.93**

The proposed system iterates through each KE "E" for each KB "b" and tries to adjust the current group – entity assignment with a new assignment. A new group "Z" is assigned to entity "E" with a probability P which is a product of two probabilities p_1 and p_2. For every group, two probabilities p_1 and p_2 are calculated. $p_1 = p(Z_b/\theta_b)$ is the proportion of entities in KB "b" that are currently assigned to group Z_b. $p_2 = p(E/Z_b, \beta)$ is the proportion of assignments to group Z_b overall KB containing the entity E. The current group – entity assignment is updated with a new group with the product probability of p_1 and p_2. In this step, the model assumes that all the existing entities – groups' assignments except the current entity are correct. This assumption is essentially the probability that group Z_b generated entity E, so the current entity's group is adjusted with new probability. After several iterations, the convergence state is achieved where the KB - groups, and group - entities distributions are informationally dense. The resulted groups are shown in Table 5, where the most coherent entities represent each group. For example, the group $Z_2 = CellComp$ will contain the entities "Cytoplasm and Nucleus" which represents the highest probabilities (Table 4).

Table 5. The resulted knowledge groups.

Groups	Entities
Group1	Translocation, Retarget
Group 2	P65, RFLAT-1, syntaxin, VAMP-2, SNAP23 P27, Kip1, IKB/MAD-3, NF-KB
Group 3	Cyclin-dependent, kinase, inhibitor, cyclin E CDK2 complex
Group 4	Binding
Group 5	Cytoplasm, nucleus
Group 6	RANTE, Gene

4   Experiments

In Sect. 4, the validity of the proposal will be tested and confirmed. Moreover, the proposal's advantages will be demonstrated through a comparative analysis.

4.1 Experimental Settings

The case study presented in this paper contracted to help users to find and understand all significant correlations and patterns in different knowledge bases. Intending to allow different exploitation of this approach by different concerned users and research organizations, the intervention consists of capitalizing the presented knowledge bases in a spark [53] container combined with Hadoop [49] for knowledge bases storage. The obtained results could be easily exploited to choose the appropriate and intelligent manner from the perspective of improving the value of a given task.

Before undertaking the experimental evaluations, clearance was obtained for the next sections. Traditional KM systems ignore the knowledge capitalization mechanism. Thus, knowledge retrieval in these systems is done by looking at every knowledge base separately. In other words, the agent should fetch in every knowledge base to get the correct response. The proposed knowledge capitalization system can be used at the top of every knowledge discovery system to make knowledge implicitly available for intelligent use, reuse, and share.

In order to demonstrate the effectiveness and efficiency of the proposed approach, three different real-world knowledge bases are used for evaluation. Notably, Mesh [34], NIF [24], and GO [7] ontologies are utilized:

- Medical Subject Headings Mesh: provide a hierarchically-organized terminology for indexing, and cataloguing of biomedical information, also distribute pharmaceutical information.
- Neuroscience Information Framework (NIF): are encoding enzymes involved in the fixation of atmospheric nitrogen into a form of nitrogen available to living organisms.
- Gene Ontology (GO): GO project is a collaborative effort to address the need for consistent descriptions of gene products in different databases: FlyBase, the Saccharomyces Genome Database, and the Mouse Genome Database.

An explanatory summary of knowledge bases appears in Table 6.

Table 6. Summary of knowledge bases.

Knowledge base	Number of triples
Mesh	1262119
NIF	124337
GO	1618739
Other OWL files	1456980

4.2   Measures and Methodology

The group coherence reflects the homogeneity for knowledge entities that form a given group. The topic coherence metric is adopted to evaluate knowledge groups. The human topic ranking is treated to be the highest standard, and consequently, a measure to the topic interpretability. Knowledge groups are judged as topics, and the knowledge entities are presented as words. The proposed approach adopts the C_V coherence measure proposed by Roder et al. [40]. Specifically, the C_V is based on four major parts. The first step is the data segmentation pairs. More formally, let $E = \{e_1, \ldots, e_N\}$ be the set of top-N knowledge entities for a given group, then $S_i = \{(E', E^*)|E' = e_i; e_i \in E; E^* = E\}$ is the set of all pairs. For example, if $E = \{e_1, e_2, e_3\}$, then the pair $S_1 = \{(E' = e_1), (E^* = \{e_1, e_2, e_3\})\}$. Douven et al. [10] assume that the segmentation measures the extent to which the subset E^* supports, or conversely undermines the subset E'. The second step recovers the probabilities of a single entity $p(e_i)$, or the joint probability of two entities $p(e_i, e_j)$, which can be estimated by their frequency over the knowledge base. The coherence measure C_V incorporates a frequency sliding window calculation by which a new virtual knowledge base is created. The window size creates a slid over the knowledge base by one-entity token per step. The final probabilities $p(e_i)$ and $p(e_i, e_j)$ are calculated from the total number of virtual knowledge bases.

Given a pair $S_i = \{E', E^*\}$, the third step calculates the confirmation measure ϕ, which reflects the strength of E^* supports E'. Similar to Aletras et al. [1], E' and E^* are represented as a means context vectors in order to capture the semantic support of all entities in E. Eq. (5) is used to create the vectors by pairing them to all entities in E. Thus, the agreement between individual entities e_i and e_j is calculated using the Eq. (6) along with normalized pointwise mutual information (NPMI), where the logarithm is smoothed by adding ϵ to $\log p(e_i, e_j)$, and γ controls the weight on higher NPMI values. The confirmation measure ϕ for a given pair S_i is obtained by calculating the cosine vector similarity of all context vectors $\phi_{S_i}(\vec{u}, \vec{e})$ (Eq. 7). The final coherence score is the arithmetic mean of all confirmation measures ϕ.

$$\vec{v}(E') = \left\{ \sum_{e_i \in E'} NMPI(e_i, e_j)^\gamma \right\}_{j=1,\ldots,|E|} \tag{5}$$

$$NMPI(e_i, e_j)^\gamma = \left(\frac{\log \frac{p(e_i, e_j) + \epsilon}{p(e_i) \cdot p(e_j)}}{-\log p(e_i, e_j) + \epsilon} \right)^\gamma \tag{6}$$

$$\phi_{S_i}(\vec{u}, \vec{e}) = \frac{\sum_{i=1}^{|E|} u_i . e_i}{\| \vec{u} \|_2 . \| \vec{e} \|_2} \tag{7}$$

Since the C_V metric evaluates the model's quality internally, the proposed approach evaluated using the PMI-Score [32], which measures the coherence of a group based on pointwise mutual information (PMI) using external sources. Besides, these external knowledge bases are model-independent, which makes the PMI-Score fair for all models. Lower PMI-scores indicates more generative models, comparing to higher values.

Given a set of N probable entities $(e_1, \cdots, e_N)$, for a group G, the PMI-Score measures the pairwise association between them:

$$PMI_{Score}(G) = \frac{1}{N(1-N)} \sum_{1<i<j<N} PMI(e_i, e_j) \tag{8}$$

$$PMI(e_i, e_j) = \log \frac{p(e_i, e_j) + \epsilon}{p(e_i)p(e_j)} \tag{9}$$

4.3 Experimental Results

In order to further verify the validity and accuracy of the proposal, this work aimed to first identify the model's parameters and metrics in terms of group coherence. The authors conducted detailed results and in-depth analysis of three different models, which revealed that: once the parameters have been modified upon, the agents were updated their parameters, and the model quality will be improved. The first evaluation goal measures the coherent of the formulated groups. In other words, how good are the constructed group according to two metrics group coherence and PMI-Scores. Therefore, the coherence phase provides the results of three different models in order to illustrate the efficiency of the shared parameters mechanism in terms of improving the model quality. Secondly, knowledge discovery and knowledge generation from the existing ones is presented through an illustrative example. In the last phase, the knowledge retrieval system, which serves as a service layer to the developed framework, permits to measure two relevant criteria - the response precision and time. These criteria reflect the strength and homogeneity of the final distributed knowledge groups.

Table 7 is revealing in several ways. First, it illustrates an evolution over the group's size, from 50 to 300. Second, interestingly, there was also a fast convergence to the stationary model, which takes three rebuilding models by an augmentation of 20% in terms of group coherence. Next, the experiments are done for the three different models. The average coherences in the first, second, and third models are 0.43, 0.72, and 0.73, respectively. Table 8 compares the PMI-Scores for the three models and demonstrates that the third model outperforms the other two models, which has a lower PMI-Score. The knowledge bases are exchanged to measure the PMI-Scores for each model. Assuming that we are using three knowledge bases, if the built model uses the two first knowledge bases, then the third knowledge base acts as an external resource for the PMI metric.

Table 7. The coherence of different models

Groups size	First model	Second model	Third model
50	0.53	0.72	0.73
100	0.43	0.72	0.72
150	0.46	0.71	0.71
200	0.51	0.70	0.70
250	0.55	0.69	0.70
300	0.59	0.69	0.69

Table 8. The PMI-Scores of different models

Groups size	First model	Second model	Third model
50	−0.36	−0.51	−0.5
100	−0.24	−0.48	−0.48
150	−0.13	−0.47	−0.47
200	−0.11	−0.45	−0.45
250	−0.09	−0.45	−0.44
300	−0.09	−0.44	−0.44

Figure 6 indicates that even if some groups in the first model produce higher coherence values, the rest of the groups are weakly correlated. In other words, the dispersion in such a model is high. Contrary to the second and the third models, which are smooth and informationally dense.

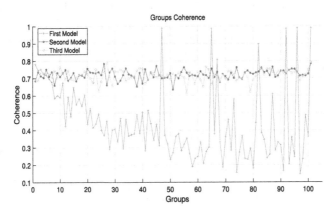

Fig. 6. Coherence over the three models.

The distributed agents use the local knowledge bases and the estimated parameters set to build their local models. However, focusing on each model

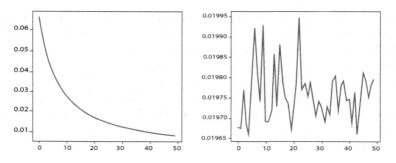

Fig. 7. Parameters distribution update over different copies.

by tuning its parameters is time and resource consuming, and with the scale of the big data context, this model's process will diverge. On the one hand, the left graph in Fig. 7 represents the first changing strategy, which gives more accurate results than the first model. On the other hand, the right graph in Fig. 7 indicates a very dense distribution comparing to the other model distribution; besides, this is the most accurate configuration for the whole system.

The knowledge capitalization framework can minimize the risk of knowledge lost, increase the system's strength to generate new knowledge, by combining the existing knowledge bases and restructuring it to be reused by different users/systems. In practice, this system was found to influence the big data value creation positively. Moreover, it highlights the need for capitalizing proven and established knowledge. Figure 8 describes a knowledge discovery example, where the two main concepts *"Memory"* and *"Memory Process"* have no direct link in the origin knowledge base. Therefore, the proposed system connects these two

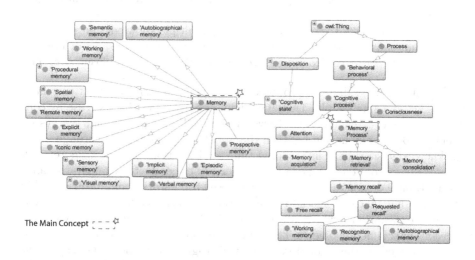

Fig. 8. Knowledge discovery example using the NIF ontology.

entities after realizing that they have common entities. Note that, concepts that are not directly connected ($e_1 = Memory$ and $e_3 = MemoryProcess$ in Fig. 9) may be indirectly connected through common concepts.

After evaluating the groups' coherence using different metrics, illustrating the importance of the shared parameters mechanism, and demonstrating the knowledge discovery task, the final step consists of inspecting these groups using the knowledge retrieval system. First of all, the following requests/queries are used by the knowledge retrieval system; they are relying on different knowledge entities from different knowledge bases:

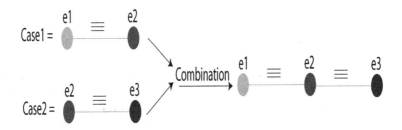

Fig. 9. Knowledge combination.

- Request 1: consists of seeking knowledge, which does not exist in all knowledge bases.
- Requests 2, 3, 4, and 5: search for one knowledge entity in different knowledge bases, omnipresent in several places (the knowledge entity belongs to various knowledge bases). For example, searching for a single knowledge entity "protein".
- Combined requests 1, 2, 3, and 4: search for multiple knowledge entities, using the same request (knowledge entities, which belong to the same or different knowledge bases). For example searching for "Protein - Cytoplasm - Retinal".

Results revealed that the proposed system could return the direct correlated knowledge in a small while. Table 9 explains the results of this use case by comparing the above ten requests. However, for real-time processing, the system offers the best combination between the update steps and speed through different knowledge streams. The response time minimization for knowledge retrieval can address various complex real-life problems. The conducted comparative analysis in Table 9 demonstrated that the proposed framework could intuitively offer different practical capabilities to improve the knowledge capitalization paradigm in specific situations, which are characterized by emergency, sensitivity, and decision-makers heterogeneity. This study's proposal offers the optimal response time compared to the ordinal systems, which ignore the knowledge capitalization step. Despite, the rebuilt models are improving during the learning process and making the optimal model more robust and accurate. Since the knowledge

Table 9. Necessary time for request responding based on request type.

Requests	Ordinal system	First model	Second model	Third model
Request 1	19.96 s	12.62 s	0.9 s	0.65 s
Request 2	20.08 s	0.17 s	0.07 s	0.059 s
Request 3	20.54 s	0.17 s	0.08 s	0.057 s
Request 4	19.70 s	0.16 s	0.07 s	0.058 s
Request 5	20.36 s	0.18 s	0.07 s	0.061 s
Combined request 1	35.96 s	0.69 s	0.08 s	0.064 s
Combined request 2	39.20 s	0.48 s	0.08 s	0.064 s
Combined request 3	43.34 s	0.64 s	0.08 s	0.065 s
Combined request 4	52.18 s	0.79 s	0.09 s	0.065 s
Search average	30.14 s	1.76 s	0.08 s	0.063 s

groups are represented as coherent knowledge entities, the clustering step of the formulated groups is omitted. In other words, the group's number and size are flexible according to the available resources.

Together these results provide important insights into the relationship between the knowledge group construction and the response time needed for their examination. Interestingly, this correlation is related to response precision, either. However, connecting users/systems to the exact and precise knowledge, they need at the time they demand it is a challenging process. The response precision is defined as returning the exact and the correct knowledge (i.e. the big data value) with the higher correlation scores. In other words, the request keywords must contribute positively to the construction of the knowledge group. The theoretical and practical value of the system precision is evaluated using a short and a long request. The short request contains the entity *"Protein"*, where the second request contains twenty-three knowledge entity including *"Protein - Inhibition - Retinal - enzymes - ..."*. The three models are inspected using these two requests. Since each model has its group formulation, however, these groups are different from one model to another. As the proposed solution is unsupervised, the authors assign the request correlated group id manually. The assignment summary is presented in Table 10.

Table 10. Long and short request assignments.

Model	Short request	Long request
First model	id_{12}	id_1
Second model	id_{50}	id_{55}
Third model	id_0	id_{78}

Table 11 summarises the response's precision analysis of different models. However, the contribution score indicates the participation of the knowledge entity to the group formulation in both directions (positive and negative). All models responded correctly with high precision, which means that the formulated knowledge groups are coherent, smooth, and understandable from the knowledge utilization perspective. On the one hand, the first model returned a noisy response by including other less correlated knowledge entities; thus, the response precision is low comparing to the two other models. Moreover, it requires a response filter to review the answer to the user request. In other words, it eliminates the weakly correlated knowledge; however, that demands extra time and resources. On the other hand, the second model returns better results than the first one, which implies that the knowledge groups are improving while the learning process goes on. Besides, this finding approves the parameter sharing strength. Finally, the third model answers the user request with the exact response and with the highest score.

It worth mentioning that the first models are successfully achieving considerable scores on the knowledge reuse task. In other words, before refreshing the models' parameters, the current models still revealing attractive performances.

Table 11. Comparing the response precision.

Request type	Model	Group Id	Score
Short request	First model	0	0.01
		8-18-64	0.25
		12	**0.5**
	Second model	**50**	**0.52**
		1	0.34
	Third Model	**0**	**0.66**
Long request	First model	0	0.02
		1	**0.51**
		$2 \rightarrow 10$	0.01
	Second model	**55**	**0.60**
		82	0.01
	Third model	**78**	**0.71**

Regarding the need for a knowledge capitalization system in the big data context, the discussed results aim at encouraging organizations to adopt the presented kind of framework at the top of any KM system. Last but not least, the offered knowledge capitalization approach helps in grouping similar knowledge entities by their internal coherence. Even if this case was applied in the big data context, it remains one of the highest contributions which push the capitalization paradigm forward. This reveals the high extensibility of the developed framework to different inputs, other than ontologies or textual knowledge bases. Besides, the shared parameters mechanism is allowing the identification of the coherent knowledge groups, improving knowledge quality, guaranteeing the response precision, and reducing the access time. Moreover, hidden relations between the resultant groups are further proposed enabling the identification of highly correlated relationships between entities in the same groups as well as for entities that belong to different groups. Accordingly, this work is initially the first to propose the shared parameters paradigm in knowledge capitalization problem with the big data context. Focusing on such a mechanism may lead to avoid knowledge loss, increase the dependency on different expertise, and make the evolution of the accumulated knowledge more difficult. Thus, the proposed approach capable of building accurate and precise groups. Given this, an essential strength of the framework is its usability in the complex environments with a massive volume of knowledge bases and a large number of models' parameters.

5   Conclusion

This paper was undertaken to design a new distributed knowledge capitalization framework and evaluate its performances in big data context. The key strength of this framework is its clearness in formulating and storing the related knowledge entities into different distributed sites. Furthermore, focusing on each model separately and tuning its parameters require more extended time and resources to find the optimal configuration; so the proposed approach uses the shared parameter mechanism driven by the group coherence metric. Mainly, it relies on this paradigm to increase the model's quality, improving knowledge entities coherence, and advancing their smoothness and density. The analysis of this additional feature extended the learning process to exciting new areas that are characterized by parameter sensitivity and heterogeneity. Alongside the preparation stage, the framework incorporates the concept of knowledge reuse via capturing the exact knowledge in due time at hand. As a result, since the formulated groups are highly coherent, the knowledge access is rapid and accurate. Besides, the framework kept the semantic relations between entities while merging different knowledge bases without redundancy. In comparison with different distributed models, the new approach proved a critical consistency and reliability in learning the highly accurate models.

In future research, the proposed framework will be extended to extract the knowledge rules that typically involve several representations and types, uniquely to identify the critical rules during the extraction process further.

References

1. Aletras, N., Stevenson, M.: Evaluating topic coherence using distributional semantics. In: Proceedings of the 10th International Conference on Computational Semantics (IWCS 2013)-Long Papers, pp. 13–22 (2013)
2. Audsley, N.C., Chan, Y., Gray, I., Wellings, A.J.: Real-time big data: the juniper approach (2014). Accepted in Reaction 2014

3. Basanta-Val, P., Fernández-García, N., Wellings, A.J., Audsley, N.C.: Improving the predictability of distributed stream processors. Future Gener. Comput. Syst. **52**, 22–36 (2015)
4. Beach, C.S., Schiefelbein, W.R.: Unstructured data: how to implement an early warning system for hidden risks. J. Account. **217**(1), 46 (2014)
5. Becerra-Fernandez, I., Sabherwal, R.: Knowledge Management: Systems and Processes. Routledge, Abingdon (2014)
6. Blei, D.M., Ng, A.Y., Jordan, M.I.: Latent Dirichlet allocation. J. Mach. Learn. Res. **3**, 993–1022 (2003)
7. Consortium, G.O.: The gene ontology (GO) database and informatics resource. Nucleic Acids Res. **32**(suppl_1), D258–D261 (2004)
8. Côrte-Real, N., Ruivo, P., Oliveira, T., Popovič, A.: Unlocking the drivers of big data analytics value in firms. J. Bus. Res. **97**, 160–173 (2019)
9. Dignum, V.: An overview of agents in knowledge management. In: Umeda, M., Wolf, A., Bartenstein, O., Geske, U., Seipel, D., Takata, O. (eds.) INAP 2005. LNCS (LNAI), vol. 4369, pp. 175–189. Springer, Heidelberg (2006). https://doi.org/10.1007/11963578_14
10. Douven, I., Meijs, W.: Measuring coherence. Synthese **156**(3), 405–425 (2007). https://doi.org/10.1007/s11229-006-9131-z
11. Dubey, R., Agrawal, P., Pathak, D., Griffiths, T.L., Efros, A.A.: Investigating human priors for playing video games. arXiv preprint arXiv:1802.10217 (2018)
12. Durupt, A., Bricogne, M., Remy, S., Troussier, N., Rowson, H., Belkadi, F.: An extended framework for knowledge modelling and reuse in reverse engineering projects. Proc. Inst. Mech. Eng. Part B J. Eng. Manuf. **233**(5), 1377–1389 (2019)
13. Esposito, C., Ficco, M., Palmieri, F., Castiglione, A.: A knowledge-based platform for big data analytics based on publish/subscribe services and stream processing. Knowl.-Based Syst. **79**, 3–17 (2015)
14. Fahey, L., Prusak, L.: The eleven deadliest sins of knowledge management. Calif. Manag. Rev. **40**(3), 265–276 (1998)
15. Fan, C., Xiao, F., Madsen, H., Wang, D.: Temporal knowledge discovery in big BAS data for building energy management. Energy Build. **109**, 75–89 (2015)
16. Gandomi, A., Haider, M.: Beyond the hype: big data concepts, methods, and analytics. Int. J. Inf. Manage. **35**(2), 137–144 (2015)
17. Gangemi, A., Recupero, D.R., Mongiovì, M., Nuzzolese, A.G., Presutti, V.: Identifying motifs for evaluating open knowledge extraction on the web. Knowl.-Based Syst. **108**, 33–41 (2016)
18. Gao, T., Chai, Y., Liu, Y.: A review of knowledge management about theoretical conception and designing approaches. Int. J. Crowd Sci. **2**(1), 42–51 (2018)
19. García-Valls, M., Basanta-Val, P.: Analyzing point-to-point DDS communication over desktop virtualization software. Comput. Stand. Inter. **49**, 11–21 (2017)
20. Gilks, W.R., Richardson, S., Spiegelhalter, D.: Markov Chain Monte Carlo in Practice. Chapman and Hall/CRC, London (1995)
21. Gonzalez, R.V.D., Martins, M.F.: Knowledge management process: a theoretical-conceptual research. Gestão & Produção **24**(2), 248–265 (2017)
22. Grau, B.C., Horrocks, I., Motik, B., Parsia, B., Patel-Schneider, P., Sattler, U.: OWL 2: the next step for OWL. Web Semant. Sci. Serv. Agents World Wide Web **6**(4), 309–322 (2008)
23. Gudivada, V.N., Baeza-Yates, R.A., Raghavan, V.V.: Big data: promises and problems. IEEE Comput. **48**(3), 20–23 (2015)

24. Gupta, A., et al.: Federated access to heterogeneous information resources in the neuroscience information framework (NIF). Neuroinformatics **6**(3), 205–217 (2008). https://doi.org/10.1007/s12021-008-9033-y
25. Hellmann, S., Auer, S.: Towards web-scale collaborative knowledge extraction. In: Gurevych, I., Kim, J. (eds.) The People's Web Meets NLP. Theory and Applications of Natural Language Processing, pp. 287–313. Springer, Heidelberg (2013). https://doi.org/10.1007/978-3-642-35085-6_11
26. Hirchoua, B., Ouhbi, B., Frikh, B.: A new knowledge capitalization framework in big data context. In: Proceedings of the 19th International Conference on Information Integration and Web-based Applications & Services, pp. 40–48. ACM (2017)
27. Hirchoua, B., Ouhbi, B., Frikh, B.: Topic hierarchies for knowledge capitalization using hierarchical Dirichlet processes in big data context. In: Ezziyyani, M. (ed.) AI2SD 2018. AISC, vol. 915, pp. 592–608. Springer, Cham (2019). https://doi.org/10.1007/978-3-030-11928-7_54
28. Intezari, A., Gressel, S.: Information and reformation in KM systems: big data and strategic decision-making. J. Knowl. Manage. **21**(1), 71–91 (2017)
29. Ling, X., Yuan, Y., Wang, D., Liu, J., Yang, J.: Joint scheduling of MapReduce jobs with servers: performance bounds and experiments. J. Parallel Distrib. Comput. **90**, 52–66 (2016)
30. Lomotey, R.K., Deters, R.: Towards knowledge discovery in big data. In: 2014 IEEE 8th International Symposium on Service Oriented System Engineering (SOSE), pp. 181–191. IEEE (2014)
31. López-Ramos, L.A., Cortés-Robles, G., Roldán-Reyes, E., Alor-Hernández, G., Sánchez-Ramírez, C.: The knowledge-based maintenance: an approach for reusing experiences in industrial systems. In: García Alcaraz, J.L., Rivera Cadavid, L., González-Ramírez, R.G., Leal Jamil, G., Chong Chong, M.G. (eds.) Best Practices in Manufacturing Processes, pp. 505–523. Springer, Cham (2019). https://doi.org/10.1007/978-3-319-99190-0_23
32. Mimno, D., Wallach, H.M., Talley, E., Leenders, M., McCallum, A.: Optimizing semantic coherence in topic models. In: Proceedings of the Conference on Empirical Methods in Natural Language Processing, pp. 262–272. Association for Computational Linguistics (2011)
33. Muñoz, E., Nickles, M.: Statistical relation cardinality bounds in knowledge bases. In: Hameurlain, A., Wagner, R., Benslimane, D., Damiani, E., Grosky, W.I. (eds.) Transactions on Large-Scale Data- and Knowledge-Centered Systems XXXIX. LNCS, vol. 11310, pp. 67–97. Springer, Heidelberg (2018). https://doi.org/10.1007/978-3-662-58415-6_3
34. Nelson, S.J., Johnston, W.D., Humphreys, B.L.: Relationships in medical subject headings (MeSH). In: Bean, C.A., Green, R. (eds.) Relationships in the Organization of Knowledge. ISKM, vol. 2, pp. 171–184. Springer, Dordrecht (2001). https://doi.org/10.1007/978-94-015-9696-1_11
35. Oramas, S., Espinosa-Anke, L., Sordo, M., Saggion, H., Serra, X.: Information extraction for knowledge base construction in the music domain. Data Knowl. Eng. **106**, 70–83 (2016)
36. Ouided, H., Tayab, L.M., Lyes, M.: Towards REX method for capitalizing the knowledge of a corporate memory. In: Czarnowski, I., Howlett, R.J., Jain, L.C. (eds.) IDT 2017. SIST, vol. 73, pp. 206–215. Springer, Cham (2018). https://doi.org/10.1007/978-3-319-59424-8_19
37. Paredes-Frigolett, H., Gomes, L.F.A.M.: A novel method for rule extraction in a knowledge-based innovation tutoring system. Knowl.-Based Syst. **92**, 183–199 (2016)

38. Perner, P.: Mining sparse and big data by case-based reasoning. Procedia Comput. Sci. **35**, 19–33 (2014)
39. Rasovska, I., Chebel-Morello, B., Zerhouni, N.: A mix method of knowledge capitalization in maintenance. J. Intell. Manuf. **19**(3), 347–359 (2008). https://doi.org/10.1007/s10845-008-0087-3
40. Röder, M., Both, A., Hinneburg, A.: Exploring the space of topic coherence measures. In: Proceedings of the Eighth ACM International Conference on Web Search and Data Mining, pp. 399–408. ACM (2015)
41. Rodriguez-Rocha, B.D., Castillo-Barrera, F.E., Lopez-Padilla, H.: Knowledge capitalization in the automotive industry using an ontology based on the ISO/TS 16949 standard. In: Electronics, Robotics and Automotive Mechanics Conference, CERMA 2009, pp. 100–106. IEEE (2009)
42. Ruiz, P.P., Foguem, B.K., Grabot, B.: Generating knowledge in maintenance from experience feedback. Knowl.-Based Syst. **68**, 4–20 (2014)
43. Sanz, S., Haupt, K., Maas, A., Jober, R., Prescott, B.: Optimization of knowledge transfer in ITER. Fusion Eng. Des. (2019). https://doi.org/10.1016/j.fusengdes.2019.02.088. http://www.sciencedirect.com/science/article/pii/S0920379619302625
44. Tichkiewitch, S.: Capitalization and reuse of forging knowledge in integrated design. In: Bernard, A., Tichkiewitch, S. (eds.) Methods and Tools for Effective Knowledge Life-Cycle-Management, pp. 479–485. Springer, Heidelberg (2008). https://doi.org/10.1007/978-3-540-78431-9_27
45. Torres-Coronas, T.: Encyclopedia of Human Resources Information Systems: Challenges in e-HRM. IGI Global, Hershey (2008)
46. Vidyasankar, K.: Batch composite transactions in stream processing. In: Hameurlain, A., Küng, J., Wagner, R., Decker, H. (eds.) Transactions on Large-Scale Data- and Knowledge-Centered Systems XXXIV. LNCS, vol. 10620, pp. 13–32. Springer, Heidelberg (2017). https://doi.org/10.1007/978-3-662-55947-5_2
47. Wang, C., Blei, D.M.: Collaborative topic modeling for recommending scientific articles. In: Proceedings of the 17th ACM SIGKDD International Conference on Knowledge Discovery and Data Mining, KDD 2011, pp. 448–456. ACM, New York (2011). https://doi.org/10.1145/2020408.2020480. http://doi.acm.org/10.1145/2020408.2020480
48. Wang, S., Noe, R.A.: Knowledge sharing: a review and directions for future research. Hum. Resour. Manag. Rev. **20**(2), 115–131 (2010)
49. White, T.: Hadoop: The Definitive Guide. O'Reilly Media, Inc., Sebastopol (2012)
50. Xing, E.P., et al.: Petuum: a new platform for distributed machine learning on big data. IEEE Trans. Big Data **1**(2), 49–67 (2015)
51. Yang, J., Kim, E., Hur, M., Cho, S., Han, M., Seo, I.: Knowledge extraction and visualization of digital design process. Expert Syst. Appl. **92**, 206–215 (2018)
52. Yang, X.: Knowledge management in big data times. In: 2015 IEEE Fifth International Conference on Big Data and Cloud Computing (BDCloud), pp. 168–171. IEEE (2015)
53. Zaharia, M., et al.: Apache spark: a unified engine for big data processing. Commun. ACM **59**(11), 56–65 (2016)
54. Zenkert, J., Klahold, A., Fathi, M.: Knowledge discovery in multidimensional knowledge representation framework. Iran J. Comput. Sci. **1**(4), 199–216 (2018). https://doi.org/10.1007/s42044-018-0019-0
55. Zhang, P., Essaid, A., Zanni-Merk, C., Cavallucci, D.: Case-based reasoning for knowledge capitalization in inventive design using latent semantic analysis. Procedia Comput. Sci. **112**, 323–332 (2017)

56. Zhang, P., Essaid, A., Zanni-Merk, C., Cavallucci, D., Ghabri, S.: Experience capitalization to support decision making in inventive problem solving. Comput. Ind. **101**, 25–40 (2018). https://doi.org/10.1016/j.compind.2018.06.001. http://www.sciencedirect.com/science/article/pii/S0166361518301210
57. Zheng, Y., Capra, L., Wolfson, O., Yang, H.: Urban computing: concepts, methodologies, and applications. ACM Trans. Intell. Syst. Technol. (TIST) **5**(3), 38 (2014)
58. Zwicklbauer, S., Seifert, C., Granitzer, M.: DoSeR - a knowledge-base-agnostic framework for entity disambiguation using semantic embeddings. In: Sack, H., Blomqvist, E., d'Aquin, M., Ghidini, C., Ponzetto, S.P., Lange, C. (eds.) ESWC 2016. LNCS, vol. 9678, pp. 182–198. Springer, Cham (2016). https://doi.org/10.1007/978-3-319-34129-3_12

DiNer - On Building Multilingual Disease-News Profiler

Sajal Rustagi[1]([✉]) and Dhaval Patel[2]

[1] Facebook Inc., London, UK
sajalrustagi1993@gmail.com
[2] IBM TJ Watson Research Center, Ossining, NY, USA
pateldha@us.ibm.com

Abstract. Disease-News Profiler aims to gather a collection of online news articles containing information related to diseases. A need for such profiler arises in epidemic intelligence where it acts as an information system for diseases. It can be used by health agencies and researchers to track any epidemic or to develop a knowledge base for diseases. Much of the existing profiling techniques have targeted specific languages like English, Arabic, Chinese, Spanish or Russian but have largely ignored many Asian and resource-poor languages. Building a multilingual disease-news profiler has a huge advantage in terms of coverage, timeliness, quality and information enrichment. In this paper we propose a novel system, DiNer for filtering and indexing of Disease-News. We have developed a language agnostic and low-resource based filtering technique which uses a Support Vector Machine based classifier to identify instances of Disease-news from any given news corpus. In this paper, we describe our novel approach of feature engineering and the development of Disease-Related corpus for training our SVM classifier. We have tested our filtering module on four languages - English, Hindi, Punjabi and Gujarati. Our filtering technique performs significantly better than the baseline-approach both in terms of F-Score($>5\%$) and recall($>50\%$) across languages.

Keywords: Disease recognition · Surveillance systems · Machine learning · Classification.

1 Introduction

Disease-News Profiler aims to gather a collection of online news articles containing information related to diseases. Such news articles could be related to any recent incidents or prevalence of an outbreak or could simply contain various facts about diseases. For example, for the disease *Dengue*, a Disease-News could be -

> *"Dengue cases have dipped further to 226 last week"* or
> *"WHO has approved World's First-Ever Dengue Vaccine".*

These articles qualify as disease-news as per our definition since the first headline discusses the number of cases in an ongoing outbreak and second headline is an information related to the vaccine that has been developed for a disease.

© Springer-Verlag GmbH Germany, part of Springer Nature 2020
A. Hameurlain and A Min Tjoa (Eds.): TLDKS XLIII, LNCS 12130, pp. 114–137, 2020.
https://doi.org/10.1007/978-3-662-62199-8_5

Disease-News Profiler helps to create a disease information system that could be used by health agencies and researchers to track any epidemic or to develop a disease related knowledge base. A very recent survey on epidemic intelligence also mentioned the useful of disease related information [15, 26].

Traditional systems that have been developed so far use indicator-based approach to collect disease related information [25] i.e. reporting of diseases and health cases by doctors, laboratories and clinics. These systems are primarily involved in collection of information related to a predefined set of attributes of diseases. As a result, traditional surveillance systems involve huge delay (about weeks) to report an incident. Additionally, these systems are unable to report new diseases or first cases of a known disease with in a short time span. This inability led to the outbreak of H1N1, 2009 and Severe Acute Respiratory Syndrome (SARS), 2003 [1]. After various global epidemics, internet based bio-surveillance became a timely resource that could handle the requirements of health authorities. Health agencies such as World Health Organizations (WHO) and US Centers for Disease Control and Prevention (CDC) even developed global news based reporting systems such as ProMED-mail[1].

There has been huge development in the field of internet based disease detection [4] which involves use of data available on internet such as search query logs [10], social media [20], news media, emails or information regarding mass gatherings [28]. Various papers [3,6,15,23,26] have illustrated the importance of developing multilingual solutions for developing repositories not only in terms of *coverage* but also in regards to *timeliness* [6] and *information enrichment* [23]. However, the majority of approaches and public surveillance systems that we explored are based on a few languages. These systems also involve the use of manual labor to filter out extracted results. Machine translation or development of lexicon and special components for each language makes these approaches more computationally intensive and high resource based. The data required for different approaches are either not commercially available or difficult to obtain. Sometimes reliability also becomes a huge issue for such data sources. In summary, our objective is to use appropriate online information sources and to design a technique which makes the proposed system:

- **Language Agnostic:** The approach that we discuss to filter out diseases related information is language agnostic in nature, as it does not make use of any linguistic properties.
- **Low Resource Based:** The proposed approach does not make use of any lemmatizers, parsers or machine translation tools and hence avoids the need for developing these components for each language. This makes the approach low-resource based and computationally feasible.
- **Freely available Data:** As discussed in the next section, we use online news media as the source of information which is freely available and easy to obtain using media news aggregators and web-monitoring techniques such as crawling and scraping. Online news is published in large number of languages which helps in availability of ample data across languages.

---

[1] http://www.promedmail.org/.

- **Reliable Information:** News Media only report facts and information related to events and incidents. It could involve biases in views related to entities. However, the system that we are trying to build avoids any biases because it relies on factual truths discussed in online news media [9].
- **Real time & fully automated:** Our approach works very well on streaming data and hence the disease-news filtered by our system could be used for real-time automatic building of disease-news repositories [22].

We propose to use online news media to obtain disease related information for any Indian language. We call the proposed system *"DiNer"*. Given a news article, DiNer identifies if it contains any disease related information using a machine-learning models. Methods that we propose for preparation of features and training corpus are language agnostic in nature as we don't make use of any language specific properties. We also demonstrate the working of the proposed methodology across four languages (English, Hindi, Punjabi and Gujarati). To summarize, the major contributions of our work are as following:

- Proposed a system "DiNer" to profile Disease-News in automated fashion.
- *Identified the problems* in existing repositories responsible for collecting news related to diseases.
- Introduced methods to develop features for capturing the properties of disease related news without using language specific properties.
- Proposed mechanism to develop training corpus of disease related news for resource-poor languages and compared this corpus to other available sources for training data.
- Evaluated the performance of trained machine learning models for various languages.

Literature review for our work is given in Sect. 2. Section 3 discusses basic architecture of proposed system. Techniques used for preparation of training data and feature development for our classifier are described in Sect. 4. Section 5 discuss SVM based model training. Experimental analysis is conducted in Sect. 6.

2   Literature Review

Table 1 gives an overview of well known diseases related systems. The earliest work related to the identification of disease related information were primarily focused on biomedical texts and reports [14]. ProMED-Mail [29] and GPHIN [7] systems make use of media sources provided by its free subscribers and specialized analysts across languages that manually filter out the news articles related to diseases. The reports generated by ProMED-mail system were directly used by EpiSPIDER [13].

MedISys [27] and HealthMap [8] use keyword based approach and make use of disease names and locations to filter out the articles related to diseases. While MedISys keeps a dictionary of disease names across languages, HealthMap is primarily based on machine translation of articles to English and has its parser

Table 1. Existing systems and their method of collecting disease related articles

Name of system	Year	# of languages	Still working	Availability
HealthMap [8]	2006	7	Yes	Website
BioCaster [5]	2006	8	No	
EpiSPIDER [13]	2004	1	No	
MedISys/PULS [27]	2004	45	Yes	No public access
GPHIN [7]	1997	9	Yes	Paid Subscription
ProMED-Mail [29]	1994	7	Yes	Subscription based

developed specially for English Language. BioCaster [5] developed ontology for each disease including its causing agents, symptoms, synonyms in English and further developed similar ontology for eight other languages (European) which were later cross linked by analysts along with the preferred terms in each language. Development of a huge in-depth cross lingual ontology for could be time-consuming and involve huge manual labour.

Romain et al. [18] have developed a state of art technique in the field of language agnostic filtering of disease related articles. Character based string matching technique has been used to determine the occurrence of disease name without the use of lemmatizers/stemmers which are not available for weak/poor languages. The technique used by Romain et al. [18] could be easily scaled up with inclusion of new weak languages but use of keyword based approach lead to poor recall. Wikipedia is available across languages but number of disease names that are available on Wikipedia for weaker languages is very low. This lead to the requirement of manual expansion of disease-names dictionary developed using Wikipedia for each language. The total number of articles categorized as disease-related by this approach is highly dependent on the size of their disease-names dictionary. It not only performs poorly for resource-poor languages where the list of all possible disease names is not available but also doesn't take into account any new diseases which gets discovered with time. Hence it leads to a need of manual update to the dictionary.

News media monitoring tools such as EMM [24], iMM [19] are used to keep an eye on how and what news media report about their organization, about an entity, about a social topic. These systems have accumulated huge amount of news information published by online news media and social media. The major contribution of these systems is in developing real time event extraction [12], disease mention recognition system [22], named entity corpus creation [17] etc.

The use of social media to track syndrome surveillance is also an interesting area of research. Interested readers can obtain a comprehensive list of existing surveillance systems from very recent review work [15, 26].

3   DiNer - Basic Architecture ,

Given a stream of news articles, DiNer automatically extracts the articles containing disease related information. In Fi. 1, we highlight three important components of DiNer system: a) Train Dataset, b) Candidate Source, and c) Diner Filtering. Train Dataset module provides a language specific corpus for training machine learning model. Candidate Source provides a stream of fresh news-articles for real time discovery of Disease-News. Diner Filtering is a core component of our work that focuses on extracting features from unstructured text to build a machine learning model.

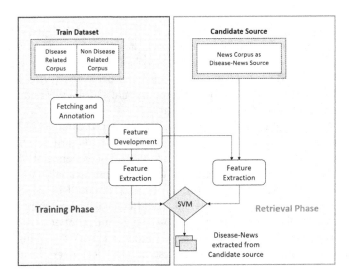

Fig. 1. Architecture of DiNer

We made two significant contributions while developing DiNer. Our first contribution is in designing a methodology to generate "Disease Related Corpus" and, the second contribution is in generating the engineered features in a low-resource and language agnostic manner which could capture the way diseases are discussed in news corpus. In Fig. 1, we have embedded two phases: Training and Scoring. In the Training Phase, we train the SVM classifier to differentiate between disease and non disease related corpus. For any given language, DiNer first trains an SVM classifier using the training data-set. The training pipeline of DiNer follow a series of steps as given follow:

$$\{Train\ Dataset \rightarrow Fetching + Annotation \rightarrow FeatureExtraction \rightarrow SVM\}$$

Our SVM classifier has been trained using different sets of training corpora that are available for a given language. By using the trained SVM classifier, we can decide whether a candidate news should be classified as Disease-News or not.

3.1   Train Dataset

To train a supervised machine learning model, we need to collect instances of both classes i.e. Disease Related (Positive) and Non Disease Related (Negative) corpora. In general, our training data consists of equal number of instances of both classes, i.e. in ratio of 50:50. In the following subsection, we discuss the process of obtaining the corpus for both disease related and non disease related information.

Disease Related Corpus. The availability of disease related corpus for a major language like English is not an issue. We noticed the existence of different types of repositories for English language such as HealthMap, IDSP, etc. However, developing such a corpus for resource-poor languages is a major issue as no such public surveillance systems have been maintained for such languages.

We identified four major sources for obtaining disease related corpus in different languages:

1. **HealthMap:** *(Only English)* HealthMap is a public surveillance system used by WHO and is hosted on web[2]. HealthMap aggregates disease-news from other reliable sources. This system has been developed for only seven major languages including English. We can obtain the entire news articles to prepare positive classes for English language.

2. **IDSP:** *(Only English)* Integrated Disease Surveillance Programme (IDSP) is another surveillance project that has been developed specific to India by National Center for Disease Control (NCDC). Various state agencies and trusted hospitals report weekly disease surveillance data. Based on the weekly report, a monthly report is manually developed and uploaded on IDSP website[3]. The reports are prepared only in English languages.

3. **Wikipedia:** *(Most Languages)* Due to topic coverage of Wikipedia, we use it as a source for obtaining various disease related articles. Wikipedia provides multilingual and cross-linked articles for most of the languages. Currently, we obtain all the articles provided in English that are covered under category *"Disease and Disorders"* and also cross linked pages for our required languages. Highlighted portion in Figure 2 illustrates the Cross Linking of Wikipedia Dengue English Article to Hindi Article.

4. **News articles with Disease Names:** *(All Languages)* This is our own method of creating disease related corpus. We manually created a basic list of disease-names for each language. We also used Google Translate and online knowledge bases for cross language translation. All the news articles containing these names of diseases are extracted and used as disease related corpus.

---

[2] http://www.healthmap.org/en/.
[3] http://idsp.nic.in/.

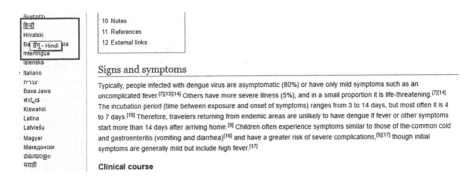

Fig. 2. Screenshot of Wikipedia dengue article and its cross-linking to Hindi article

Non Disease Related Corpus. Our initial experiments performed with English language illustrated that only 5819 out of 218712 articles contained name of any diseases i.e. only 2.66%. In machine learning community having very few samples from one class is known as class imbalance [21]. It is known that building model for such imbalanced data-set is very difficult. The news that we collect on daily basis from news websites consists of a variety of topics including politics, sports, business, economics etc. We can observe that the instances of Disease-news that we obtain from daily news is very few and this corpus can be easily considered as "Non-Disease Related Corpus". This corpus can be easily created for any languages as the dedicated news websites and crawlers are easily available.

3.2 Candidate Source

For a given language, our DiNer system requires some source from where information related to diseases could be extracted i.e. a source to provide candidates to classify. Information available on social media, news media, biomedical texts, various clinical texts and reports could act as a candidate source. In this paper, we choose news media as our candidate source due to reliability, factual correctness, volume, availability and ease of extraction.

We leveraged our intelligent crawling system, namely iMM [19] for the extraction of news articles. These crawlers visit pre-identified set of website at regular interval (15 min) and extract all the news articles that were published in that duration. This procedure was followed for each language and each news publishing website to obtain candidates for developing real time data collection for candidate source.

3.3 DiNer Filtering

DiNer filtering module primarily consists of three steps: 1) Fetching and Annotation, 2) Feature Development, and 3) Feature Extraction. Each module is explained in detail in the following subsection.

Fetching and Annotation. Disease related corpus is derived from two different sources i.e. "Wikipedia" and "News Articles with Disease Names" for all languages. Apart from these, we also use two other sources i.e. "HealthMap" and "IDSP" for English language. We have implemented specialized scrappers [2,11], PDF parsers and BoilerPlate API's to extract articles and reports [16]. Due to minuscule occurrence of disease related articles in daily news, "Non Disease Related Corpus" is fetched from news publishing website using crawlers. These two different types of corpus are annotated with appropriate classes i.e. disease-related or not based on the source of their collection.

Feature Development. The input to this module consists of equal number of instances of both classes i.e. same number of articles belonging to classes Disease Related and Non Disease Related. As the method that we develop is low resource based, we don't make use of any stemmers or lemmatizers. Articles are processed for feature engineering in their natural form. As the process of extraction of frequently occurring unigrams is standard for most of the languages under consideration, we make use of this language agnostic property to prepare feature vector for our classifier. We suggest two different language agnostic methods to prepare feature vectors given as:

- **Unbiased:** *(Entire Training Corpus)* In this method, top-K frequently occurring unigrams are extracted from entire training dataset (Disease and Non Disease) which contains equal number of instances of each. As a result, unigrams that are extracted capture the properties and frequency distribution of both the corpora. This method of feature development has no biases in treatment of instances of both the classes.
- **Biased:** *(Only Disease Related Corpus)* In this method, top-K frequently occurring unigrams are extracted from disease related corpus i.e. only the instances belonging to Class Disease-Related. As a result, unigrams that are extracted capture the properties and distribution of disease related articles. This method of feature engineering is biased to focus to instances of positive class i.e. articles belonging to disease-related corpus

We compare the performance of both the methods of feature development for different languages in our experimental work. Both the methods are compared in terms of various parameters such as recall, minimal size of training data-sets required and change in accuracy with variation in size of feature vector i.e. value of K.

Feature Extraction. This module is needed in both workflow execution of DiNer Filtering. Given the feature developed and corpora, this module is responsible for preparation of K-sized Boolean vector for top K unigrams extracted in previous section. The Boolean values in feature vector prepared for each article is marked as True or False based on the occurrence of unigram in the article corresponding to each of K features developed i.e. K unigrams extracted in Feature Development module.

3.4   Execution Phases of DiNer Filtering Classifier

Similar to all machine learning approaches, DiNer filtering step also work in two different phases: Training and Scoring. Training data is provided to train our classifier during training phase. Once trained, this classifier is used to extract Disease-News from our candidate source during the Scoring Phase in order to build Disease-News Repository. Two phases of our DiNer filtering steps are given as follows:

- **Training phase:** For inclusion of Disease-news for a new language to our Disease-News Repository using DiNer, this phase needs to be executed only once. We need to prepare the training data-set i.e. instances of both classes, Disease Related Corpus and Non Disease Related Corpus using Fetching and Annotation module. Once prepared, this training data-set is used to develop features for our feature vector i.e. extraction of frequently occurring unigrams from our training data-set. Feature extraction module is used to develop feature vector which is given as input to our classifier as training feature vector.
- **Retrieval/Scoring Phase:** Once the classifier is trained during Training phase, articles from candidate source are given as an input to our feature extraction module. Using features developed during the training phase i.e. frequently occurring unigrams, occurrence of these unigrams in the candidate is evaluated in order to develop boolean feature vector. This feature vector can be used by our classifier to predict whether input instance belong to class of Disease-News or not.

4   Experiments - Fetching, Annotation and Feature Development

In this section, we describe the outcome of our data collection method. We prepare training corpus for four different languages – *English, Hindi, Punjabi and Gujarati.* We use first two letters of each of the four languages to denote the language specific corpus, For example English (En), Hindi (Hi), Punjabi (Pu) and Gujarati (Gu). The training corpus is prepared using four different sources, namely HealthMap (denoted as Hm), IDSP, Wikipedia (denoted as Wk) and News Articles with Disease Name (denoted as NwDN). For English language, we extract training data from all the sources. For the other three languages, we extract our training data from only two sources i.e. Wikipedia and News Articles with Disease Names.

Figure 3 gives an overview of data collected from different sources along with the number of instances obtained. We can clearly see that the number of disease related articles for a language other than English is very less. Disease related English news articles are downloaded directly from HealthMap, ProMed-Mail and IDSP website. In our setting, HealthMap contributed more than 350k disease related news articles, whereas India specific IDSP provided around 10k articles.

Wikipedia (Wk) articles under "Disease and Symptoms" category is available for all four languages. Again, we extracted huge number of articles from Wikipedia for English.

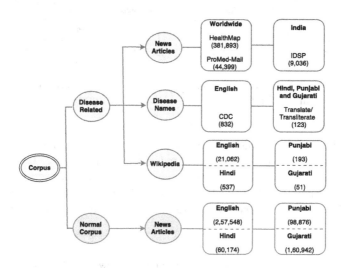

Fig. 3. Overview of data collected

For extraction of news articles containing disease names, we obtain a news corpus specific to a given language and then used a list of pre-identified disease names to obtain articles containing names of diseases. Disease names for English language are obtained from CDC[4] and for other languages translation and transliterations tools were used (Google Translate[5]/Transliterate[6]). Figure 4 gives samples of translation and transliteration of some well known disease names as provided by Google and other knowledge sources such as Shabdkosh[7]. It can be observed that for some diseases like fever both these transformations result in actual name of the disease in Hindi. For diseases like cold, meningitis or smallpox, only one of these lead to viable disease name(wrong marked with red) and for diseases such as dengue or malaria, both give the same output. As a result there is a need of manual processing of conversions obtained to create a basic list of disease names in each language. Some of sample disease names manually identified for all four languages are given in Fig. 5. In summary, we collected 800+ disease names (See Fig. 3) in English and obtained their name in other language.

Manually identified disease names are further used to extract disease-related news articles. The news articles that are obtained based on the occurrence of name of diseases are labeled as "*News Articles containing disease names,*

---

[4] http://www.cdc.gov/diseasesconditions/.
[5] https://translate.google.co.in/.
[6] https://www.google.com/inputtools/try/.
[7] http://www.shabdkosh.com/.

English Name	Translation	Transliteration
Fever	बुखार	फीवर
Smallpox	चेचक	स्मॉलपॉक्स
Dengue	डेंगू	डेंगू
Meningitis	दिमागी बुखार	मेनन्जाइटिस
Cold	ठंड	कोल्ड

English	Hindi	Punjabi	Gujarati
Chickenpox	चेचक	ਚੇਚਕ	અછબડા
Diarrhea	दस्त	ਦਸਤ	ઝાડા
Hepatitis B	हेपेटाइटिस बी	ਹੈਪੇਟਾਈਟਿਸ ਬੀ	હીપેટાઇટિસ બી
Cholera	हैज़ा	ਹੈਜ਼ਾ	કોલેરા
Herpes	दाद	ਹਰਪੀਸ	હર્પીસ

Fig. 4. Some diseases and their translation/transliterations in Hindi

Fig. 5. Some diseases and their translation/transliterations

$NwDN$". The number of disease names manually identified for each languages along with instances of NwDN extracted is given in Table 2. Out of 198708 English news articles using 95 disease names, 5819 articles were extracted as instances of $[En]_{NwDN}$ based on occurrence of these diseases in article. Similarly 524, 1091 and 1461 articles were extracted for Hindi, Punjabi and Gujarati respectively.

Table 2. Number of diseases identified and news articles extracted

Language	Notation	Total Diseases	Total Articles	Articles with disease names
English	$[En]_{NwDN}$	95	198708	5819
Hindi	$[Hi]_{NwDN}$	253	40173	524
Punjabi	$[Pu]_{NwDN}$	130	78876	1091
Gujarati	$[Gu]_{NwDN}$	188	60471	1461

All new articles other than those belonging to disease related corpus are considered as non disease-related corpus (Nw). Using articles belonging to two different classes, we prepared 10 different training data-sets. $[En]_{Nw}^{Wk}$ represents data-set of Wikipedia based disease-related corpus and news based non disease-related corpus for English language. The total number of instances of articles in each data-set (50:50 ratio for both classes) is given in Table 3. $[En]_{Nw}^{Wk}$ data-set consists of 42122 articles with 21056 instances from both Wikipedia and News Corpus (50:50).

Feature Development. We applied feature development (Unbiased and Biased) on the ten data-sets given in Table 3. We noticed a significant difference between the top K frequently occurring unigrams as we vary value of K from 1 to 1000 when using $[En]_{Nw}^{Hm}$ data-set. A high difference suggests that both the approaches take different features to build the model. From Fig. 6, we can observe that there is significant difference of around 20% in features obtained using both methodologies

Table 3. Different data-sets prepared and their number of instance

Language	Disease-related Corpus	Non disease Related corpus	Notation Notation	Total Instances
English	Wk	News	$[En]_{Nw}^{Wk}$	42122
English	Hm	News Articles	$[En]_{Nw}^{Hm}$	140062
English	IDSP	News Articles	$[En]_{Nw}^{IDSP}$	19246
English	NwDN	News Articles	$[En]_{Nw}^{NwDN}$	11638
Hindi	Wk	News Articles	$[Hi]_{Nw}^{Wk}$	1078
Hindi	NwDN	News Articles	$[Hi]_{Nw}^{NwDN}$	1048
Punjabi	Wk	News Articles	$[Pu]_{Nw}^{Wk}$	386
Punjabi	NwDN	News Articles	$[Pu]_{Nw}^{NwDN}$	2182
Gujarati	Wk	News Articles	$[Gu]_{Nw}^{Wk}$	102
Gujarati	NwDN	News Articles	$[Gu]_{Nw}^{NwDN}$	2922

which also gives huge difference in performance. Various experiments related to performance of both the methods have been demonstrated where we also make an important observation that there are two significant values of K for these methods where one outperforms the other. These values of K are identified as 100 and 1000. Therefore, we perform all the experiments related to development and testing of our model classifier over both values of K.

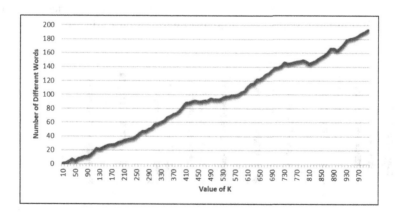

Fig. 6. Difference in Top K occurring words obtained from both methodologies

5   DiNer Filtering - Model Training

In order to filter Disease-News from news corpus in DiNer filtering step, we make use of binary classification and train classifier over feature vector developed using the training data-set. Using this classifier we can make predictions over unseen news corpus to extract disease related news in order to build our Disease-News Profiler. In this section we discuss performance of various classifiers on our train data-set, parameters for best performance of our SVM Classifier and training of our model in details.

After preparing the training data-set, we extract the features from each instance of training set to obtain training feature vector. Feature consists of boolean values based on whether a unigram occur in our instance or not. This training vector is then fed to our classifier for training and learning the distribution of Disease-Related Articles. So we need to train various types of classifiers in order to get the classifier that could give best classification over our data. To differentiate and understand the performance of each classifier, we use 10-fold cross validation accuracy as an evaluation metric to compare results from our trained classifiers.

5.1 Classifiers Comparison

Different types of classifiers can be used for binary classification of our news instances into Disease-Related and Non Disease-Related classes. The classifiers that are fairly common to use for binary classification are - Two Class SVM Classifier, Naive Bayes Classifier, Decision Tree, Random Forests, One Class SVM, and C4.5. Details related to SVM classifier are given in next section.

For comparing the performance of these classifiers, we setup an experiment using 5000 instances from the data-set $[En]_{Nw}^{Hm}$ and value of K as 1000 with biased method for feature development. These parameters were chosen for the experiments on the basis of observation that there was no significant variation in accuracy difference among the classifiers with variation in parameters.

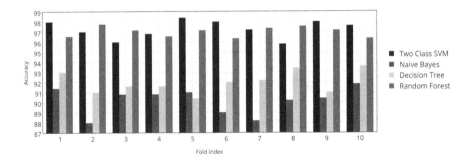

Fig. 7. Accuracy(in %) across 10 folds of training set

Figure 7 shows accuracy that we obtain for these classifiers along with each fold for 10-fold cross validation set. The average 10-fold cross validation accuracy for all the classifiers are given in Table 4. As we can observe from the Table 4, Two Class SVM outperforms all the other model classifiers with the 10-fold cross validation accuracy of 97.28%. Random Forest also performs quite well on our training set with accuracy of around 97%. All other classifiers such as Naive Bayes and Decision Tree gives better performance than One Class SVM and C4.5 but still performs poorly when compared to Two Class SVM classifier.

Based on experiment performed using different classifiers, we determine that we need to use Two Class SVM as the classifier in DiNer filtering step. For Two Class SVM classifier, we also need to choose a kernel that would most accurately fit our training data-set. With the same experimental setup, We compared performance of SVM classifiers using different kernels which is given in Table 5.

Table 4. Accuracy using different classifiers

Type of classifier	Accuracy
Two Class SVM	97.28
Random Forest	97
Decision Tree	91.98
Naive Bayes	90.16
C4.5 Algorithm	50
One Class SVM	35.38

Table 5. Accuracy using different SVM kernels

Type of kernel	Accuracy
Radial	97.28
Linear	97.02
Sigmoid	96.12
Polynomial	53.76

Based on values obtained in Table 5, we can determine that Radial Kernel function for SVM classifier gives the best fit for our training data-set. Linear kernel also performs quite well on our training data-set. Since Radial Kernel is generally used as the default for SVM classifiers and could easily work for most complex data points, ee choose Radial Kernel as our choice for kernel function in SVM classifier.

5.2   Tuning of Parameters

There are two important parameters related to SVM classifier using RBF kernel function, C and γ. C or Cost is defined as the penalty for mis-classification of training data points. With increase in C, the number of mis-classified data points goes on decreasing but this also leads to over-fitting of our classifier. As a result we get a classifier with low bias and high variance. γ or Gamma is a parameter used in radial kernel functions that decides the influence of one data point in predicting the class of another data point. Smaller value of gamma leads to low bias and high variance which that data points have lower influence over one another.

Using the same experimental setup, we used grid search to tune our parameters Cost and Gamma. In this technique we vary the values of our Cost parameter from 2^{-1} to 2^4 and Gamma parameter from 10^{-6} to 10^1 to train our SVM classifier using RBF kernel and then we calculate 10-fold cross validation accuracy for each value of parameter. The 10-fold cross validation accuracy obtained for each value of Cost and Gamma parameter are plotted in Fig. 8.

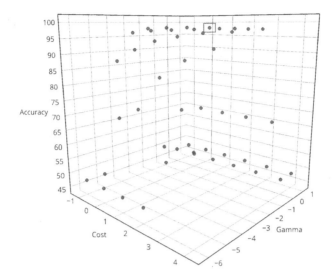

Fig. 8. 10-fold cross Validation Accuracy(in %) Vs Gamma(log10) Vs Cost(log2)

Based on values obtained for accuracy over different parameters, we chose (Cost, Gamma) parameters as (4, 0.01) which resulted in 10-fold cross validation accuracy of 98.22%.

5.3   Training of Classifiers

We prepared ten types of data-sets over four different languages. These data-sets were used as a training data-set to train our SVM classifiers using the parameters obtained in previous section. Recall, we have two different methods of feature development and two significant values of K i.e. 100 and 1000. To compare the performance of both biased and unbiased method of feature development over different data-sets, we prepared SVM classifiers for each of these data-sets using both the values of K and both the methods.

Some of the features along with weights assigned by SVM classifiers for all the four languages are given in Fig. 9. These classifiers are prepared using K = 1000, news with disease name(NwDN) as a source for disease related corpus and biased method of feature development.

As we can observe from Fig. 9, different unigrams (features) and their translations have been assigned different weights across different languages. Words related to diseases such as *Case, Health and Disease* are assigned positive (+) weights as their presence in an article indicates higher probability of article being an instance of Disease-News. Similarly fairly common words like *Said* and *People* are more prevalent in non disease related corpus and have been assigned negative (-) weights by classifiers. Higher absolute feature weight indicate a higher weightage in determining class of instance given as input. We can also make

English	Weights	Hindi	Weights	Punjabi	Weights	Gujarati	Weights
Said	-56.78	कहा	-27.03	ਕਿਹਾ	-3.91	જણાવ્યું	-20.21
Health	128.54	स्वास्थ्य	117.07	ਸਿਹਤ	175.30	આરોગ્ય	42.00
Case	43.85	मामले	4.05	ਕੇਸ	-1.39	કેસ	12.78
People	-15.75	लोगों	15.66	ਲੋਕਾਂ	40.51	લોકો	-0.72
Disease	145.54	बीमारी	119.50	ਬਿਮਾਰੀ	83.98	રોગ	151.51

Fig. 9. Sample of feature weights assigned by SVM classifiers across 4 languages

an observation that weights of most of the unigrams such as *Said, Health* and *Disease* don't show much variation across languages.

For each data-set, we needed to prepare four types of classifiers using values of K as (100, 1000) and method of feature development as (Biased, Unbiased). As a result, we prepared forty classifiers across four languages.

Table 6. 10-fold cross validation accuracy for SVM classifier developed

Data-sets	Biased		Unbiased	
	K = 100	K = 1000	K = 100	K = 1000
$[En]_{Nw}^{Hm}$	96.402	98.905	97.655	**99.775**
$[En]_{Nw}^{IDSP}$	**99.987**	99.870	99.927	99.974
$[En]_{Nw}^{Wk}$	99.556	99.938	100	**100**
$[En]_{Nw}^{NwDN}$	91.192	93.899	90.780	**96.176**
$[Hi]_{Nw}^{Wk}$	**99.314**	98.703	97.314	99.074
$[Hi]_{Nw}^{NwDN}$	**88.937**	87.599	83.016	85.783
$[Pu]_{Nw}^{Wk}$	**99.480**	98.178	98.472	98.711
$[Pu]_{Nw}^{NwDN}$	**89.457**	84.782	88.314	84.280
$[Gu]_{Nw}^{Wk}$	**100**	100	100	100
$[Gu]_{Nw}^{NwDN}$	**79.943**	78.554	77.585	79.875

Using 10-fold Cross validation accuracy for SVM classifiers as given in Table 6, we observe that Wk based SVM classifiers performed better than the classifier based on other data-sets. This is due to smaller size of the training data-set and significant linguistic difference in articles belonging to two classes. Similarly IDSP based articles are manually curated using fixed template which make them easier to distinguish from news articles and give higher accuracy values for classifier based on IDSP dataset.

NwDN and Nw based data-sets have variety of topics and discussions which make them significantly similar and lead to poor performance as compared to other classifiers. Hm provide news articles and reports that have been manually identified as belonging to Disease-Related class and consist of news article with single discussion as compared to topic-rich non Disease-Related news articles. Therefore Hm based SVM classifiers perform better as compared to NwDN but poorer than Wk and IDSP based classes.

In summary, our proposed method of corpus creation i.e. NwDN gives poorer training accuracy than other available methods e.g. using Wk articles. But we would observe in next section that Wk based SVM classifiers fail when used for extraction of Disease-News.

As marked in bold in Table 6, for most of the data-sets (70%) SVM classifier prepared with *Biased* method of feature development and using value of K (i.e. length of feature vector) as 100 performs better in terms of 10-fold cross validation accuracy than other configurations. We can also observe that for biased method, cross validation accuracy decreases with increase in K and for unbiased method it increases with value of K. We also perform experiments related to variation in Accuracy with size of feature vector for both biased and unbiased methods.

The difference in SVM weight distribution of normal news corpus and disease-news corpus using our trained SVM classifier can be observed in Fig. 10. Kindly note that the word cloud is obtained using normalized SVM weights as a feature, not the frequency of unigram occurrence. For example, the SVM weight of word "said" is highest for the both corpus, but word "report", "health", "disease", infect has more SVM weights in disease related corpus. As a result, their font size is bigger for the word cloud on right side. This ascertains that instances which are extracted using our classifier have information related to diseases.

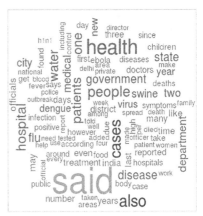

Fig. 10. Word clouds of normal news corpus (Left) and extracted disease-news (Right). The SVM weights for some subset of words in the right side Word Cloud are health (0.007), said (0.013), cases (0.006), etc.

6   DiNer Filtering - Experimental Results

In Sect. 5, we trained our SVM classifiers using ten different data-sets, values of K as (100, 1000) and both biased and unbiased method of feature development. In this section, we perform various experiments related to our SVM classifiers in order to determine their performance in extraction of Disease-News from news corpus. We also discuss some experiments performed using both methods of feature development to determine the size of training data-set needed to train our classifiers and variation in Accuracy with size of feature vector.

6.1   Performance of SVM Classifiers

In order to compare performance of classifiers in filtering of Disease-News from News Corpus, we created a test set of 20000 news articles which were not used in the training of classifiers. These trained SVM classifiers were then used to predict the class of test set instances. To compare our system against state of art, we also use baseline to compare the performance of our classifiers.

Baseline for Comparison. The technique developed by Lejeune et al. [18] is considered state of the art in extracting disease related news from news corpus. Using a predefined list of disease names mostly obtained from Wikipedia, they use keyword based approach i.e. occurrence of disease name in news article to classify it as Disease-News. We use this approach as our baseline technique i.e. an input instance is classified as Disease-News if it contains any Disease name defined in our manually prepared list. We acknowledge that recent developments in Automation in AI can be useful to build more accurate machine learning model, however, the corpus preparation and the feature engineering cannot be fully automated.

Preliminary Experiments Using Test Set. Using our classifiers developed and baseline approach, we predict the class for each of 20000 instances in our test set. The number of articles that are extracted using these approaches are demonstrated in Table 7.

As we can observe that number of instances that were extracted using IDSP and Wikipedia articles is fairly lower than $[Gu]_{Nw}^{Wk}$ and $[En]_{Nw}^{Wk}$. The reason behind this exceptional behaviour for these two data-sets is attributed to a fewer number of instances in training data-set and non convergence of their classifier during training. Classifiers using IDSP perform far below our baseline approach and fails in extraction of Disease-News. Classifier using Wk, Hm and NwDN were able to extract instances of disease news comparable to our baseline approach.

We also make an observation that classifiers prepared with biased method of feature development and $K = 100$ were able to extract maximum number of instances for each data-set. In order to assure that our classifiers developed using NwDN were able to extract the articles containing disease names, we also perform another experiment to compare the number of instances that contain disease

Table 7. Number of disease-news identified from test set

Data-sets	Biased		Unbiased	
	K = 100	K = 1000	K = 100	K = 1000
$[En]_{Nw}^{Hm}$	823	2766	4142	**10562**
$[En]_{Nw}^{IDSP}$	**33**	2	29	20
$[En]_{Nw}^{Wk}$	134	51	20000	**20000**
$[En]_{Nw}^{NwDN}$	**1803**	1172	1797	820
Baseline(En)	612			
$[Hi]_{Nw}^{Wk}$	**463**	80	s 388	63
$[Hi]_{Nw}^{NwDN}$	1361	**2188**	1732	1354
Baseline(Hi)	289			
$[Pu]_{Nw}^{Wk}$	**221**	0	74	2
$[Pu]_{Nw}^{NwDN}$	**1244**	808	1168	766
Baseline(Pu)	248			
$[Gu]_{Nw}^{Wk}$	**18509**	18508	18509	18508
$[Gu]_{Nw}^{NwDN}$	**2227**	2009	1762	1977
Baseline(Gu)	502			

names and were extracted by using our classifier in Table 8. We can observe that most of the instances(>80%) that contain names of diseases were also identified as Disease-Related by our classifiers developed. Among these classifiers, the one using biased method of feature development and K = 100 were able to extract more number of articles containing Disease Names for different languages. This experiment gives us an idea of type of articles that are identified as Disease-News by our classifiers.

Table 8. Number of instances containing Disease-names extracted by SVM

Data-set	Test instances with disease-names	Biased		Unbiased	
		K = 100	K = 1000	K = 100	K = 1000
$[En]_{Nw}^{NwDN}$	612	**407** (66.5%)	381	386	294
$[Hi]_{Nw}^{NwDN}$	289	**247** (85.4%)	244	228	239
$[Pu]_{Nw}^{NwDN}$	248	**248** (100.0%)	197	212	197
$[Gu]_{Nw}^{NwDN}$	502	339	**397** (79.08%)	315	381

Evaluation Metrics. Preliminary experiments using Test Set give us an idea of the performance of classifiers developed against baseline approach but to actually compare the approaches, we need to define an evaluation metric. In this paper we define our criteria for evaluation as **F1-Score** and **Recall**.

Comparison of Performance. In order to evaluate the performance of our developed classifiers and the baseline approach, we annotate instances in *Test Set* that were used for extraction of Disease-News by these approaches. We perform annotation of articles for two languages - *English and Hindi* to compare the performance of these approaches across languages. For annotation of articles in our Test Set, we use two different methods.

- **Manual Annotation:** We performed random weighted selection of 1,000 articles from 20,000 articles in Test Set for manual annotation. There are few($<$10%) instances of disease news in normal news corpus. So to evaluate the performance of these approaches it is more relevant to compare their prediction on these few instances. In order to identify these instances, probability value i.e. weight is assigned to each article on the basis of number of classifiers (including baseline approach) that classify it as Disease-News.
- **Crowdsourced Annotation:** We performed random weighted selection of 100 articles from 20,000 articles in Test Set for crowdsourced annotation in similar manner as mentioned above. Each annotator was asked to carefully read 3 articles (out of 100) and decide if they are related to diseases or not. We collected around 100 responses for both the languages i.e. 3 annotations per instance and each article was marked with the class receiving maximum number of response.

As most of the articles ($>$95%) that were annotated using crowdsourcing were assigned same class by manual annotation. The F1-Score and Recall values that were obtained using both the annotation methods were significantly similar. Results obtained using English corpus are given in Table 9 and Hindi corpus are given in Table 10.

Table 9. F-score and recall for English corpus

Data-sets	Measures	Biased		Unbiased	
		K = 100	K = 1000	K = 100	K = 1000
$[En]_{Nw}^{Hm}$	F-score	**57.021**	45.669	39.826	26.765
	Recall	58.771	76.315	80.701	**94.376**
$[En]_{Nw}^{Wk}$	F-score	**10.606**	3.333	-	-
	Recall	**6.140**	1.754	-	-
$[En]_{Nw}^{NwDN}$	F-score	**64.886** (5.16%)	61.538	54.819	53.846
	Recall	**80.701** (52.52%)	73.584	79.824	55.263
Baseline(En)	F-score	61.70			
	Recall	52.91			

We can observe in Table 9 that using NwDN data-set as training corpus, our biased method of feature development and K = 100 we get improvement in F-measure of 5.16% and Recall of 52.52% when compared to baseline approach.

Table 10. F-score and recall for Hindi corpus

Datasets	Measures	Biased		Unbiased	
		K = 100	K = 1000	K = 100	K = 1000
$[Hi]_{Nw}^{Wk}$	F-score	**13.164**	10.828	11.518	6.514
	Recall	**9.629**	6.296	8.148	3.703
$[Hi]_{Nw}^{NwDN}$	F-score	**63.428** (5.48%)	49.045	60.583	62.668
	Recall	<u>82.222</u> (60.86%)	**95.185**	88.518	94.814
Baseline(Hi)	F-score	<u>60.130</u>			
	Recall	<u>51.111</u>			

Classifiers using other corpora i.e. Hm or Wk could not perform as well as our proposed method of creation of training data-set(NwDN). Biased method of feature development gave better results than Unbiased method and similarly using K = 100 gave higher Recall and F-score values when compared to K = 1000.

Similar results could also be observed when used with a Hindi corpus as illustrated in Table 10 which indicates that this technique gives better performance over baseline approach across languages as well. For a classifier prepared using NwDN data-set, biased method and K = 100 we get improvement in F-score of 5.48% and Recall of 60.86%.

6.2   Variation in Performance

In this section, we perform various experiments in order to examine variation in performance with size of feature vector and to determine the minimum number of instances required to train our SVM classifiers using both biased and unbiased method of feature development.

Size of Feature Vector. The SVM classifiers discussed in previous sections were developed using size of feature vector i.e. values of K as 100 and 1000. Reason behind choice of these values can be concluded based on Fig. 11 which has been developed using 2500 instances of $[Gu]_{Nw}^{NwDN}$ as training dataset. For values of K below 100, Biased technique of feature development outperforms the Unbiased technique and for values of K above 100, classifier using Unbiased technique gives better performance.

It can also be observed in Fig. 11 that for feature vector size ¿ 100, the accuracy of SVM classifiers using Biased Technique reduces significantly with its maximum value of accuracy at K = 100. The reason behind this decline in performance could be attributed to over-fitting of our trained classifier. For Unbiased technique there is no significant change in accuracy for values of K ¿ 100 with its maximum performance around K = 1000. We also observe similar behaviour for classifiers prepared using other corpora and due to this exceptional behaviour at K = 100 and 1000, we perform all the experiments using these values for both Biased and Unbiased methods of feature development.

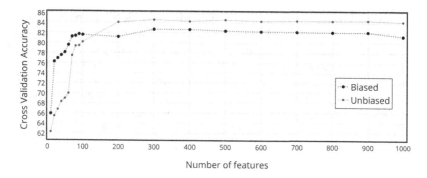

Fig. 11. Accuracy(in %) using different values of K

Size of Training Data-set. This experiment is performed to determine minimum size of training data required to train our classifiers for both methods of feature development. Using value of K as 100 and instances of $[En]_{Nw}^{NwDN}$ to train our classifier, we vary size of our training data from 10 to 100000. As the variation in performance for both the classifiers becomes negligible above 1000, we only demonstrate variation in training data from 10–1000 in Fig. 12.

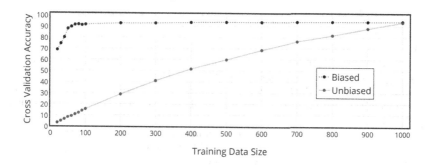

Fig. 12. Accuracy(in %) using different sizes of training data

As illustrated in Fig. 12, For smaller size of training data(<1000) Biased method gives far better results as compared to Unbiased method but for training data with number of articles > 1000, both the techniques give fairly comparable results. It can also be concluded that for Biased and Unbiased technique, minimum size of training data is around 100 and 1000 respectively to get fairly accurate results.

7   Conclusion and Future Work

We proposed a system called "DiNeR" to build and index Disease-News Profiler which tackles the problems existing in current systems responsible for collecting news related to diseases. We introduced methods to develop features that capture the properties of disease related news without using language specific properties. We also propose mechanism to develop training corpus of disease related news for resource-poor languages and compare the performance. Our filtering technique performs significantly better than baseline approach both in terms of F-Score($>$ +5%) and Recall($> +50$%) and is able to identify Disease-News from News Corpus without depending on completeness of any external knowledge source. Filtering approach of DiNeR is language agnostic and low-resource based which means this phase can be extended to all the languages without any significant effort.

Acknowledgment. We would also like to show our gratitude to the institution IIT Roorkee for providing resources to conduct this research and thank our colleagues from IIT Roorkee who provided insight and expertise that greatly assisted the research.

References

1. Al-Tawfiq, J.A., Zumla, A., Gautret, P., Gray, G.C., Hui, D.S., Al-Rabeeah, A.A., Memish, Z.A.: Surveillance for emerging respiratory viruses. Lancet. Infect. Dis **14**(10), 992–1000 (2014)
2. Barua, J., Patel, D., Goyal, V.: Tide: template-independent discourse data extraction. In: Big Data Analytics and Knowledge Discovery - 17th International Conference, DaWaK 2015, Valencia, Spain, 1–4 September, 2015, Proceedings, pp. 149–162 (2015)
3. Brixtel, R., Lejeune, G., Doucet, A., Lucas, N.: Any language early detection of epidemic diseases from web news streams. In: 2013 IEEE International Conference on Healthcare Informatics (ICHI), pp. 159–168. IEEE (2013)
4. BBrownstein, J.S., Freifeld, C.C., Madoff, L.C.: Digital disease detection—harnessing the web for public health surveillance. New England J. Med. **360**(21), 2153–2157 (2009)
5. Collier, N., et al.: Biocaster: detecting public health rumors with a web-based text mining system. Bioinformatics **24**(24), 2940–2941 (2008)
6. Collier, N., et al.: A multilingual ontology for infectious disease surveillance: rationale, design and challenges. Lang. Resour. Eval. **40**(3–4), 405–413 (2006)
7. Dion, M., AbdelMalik, P., Mawudeku, A.: Big data and the global public health intelligence network (GPHIN). Can. Commun. Dis. Rep. **41**(9), 209 (2015)
8. Freifeld, C.C., Mandl, K.D., Reis, B.Y., Brownstein, J.S.: Healthmap: global infectious disease monitoring through automated classification and visualization of internet media reports. J. Am. Med. Inform. Assoc. **15**(2), 150–157 (2008)
9. Garg, A., Syal, V., Gudlani, P., Patel, D.: Mining credible and relevant news from social networks. In: Big Data Analytics - 5th International Conference, BDA 2017, Hyderabad, India, 12–15 December, 2017, Proceedings, pp. 90–102 (2017)
10. Ginsberg, J., Mohebbi, M.H., Patel, R.S., Brammer, L., Smolinski, M.S., Brilliant, L.: Detecting influenza epidemics using search engine query data. Nature **457**(7232), 1012–1014 (2009)
11. Gupta, K., Mittal, V., Bishnoi, B., Maheshwari, S., Patel, D.: Act: accuracy-aware crawling techniques for cloud-crawler. World Wide Web **19**(1), 69–88 (2016)
12. Gupta, S., Patel, D.: Ne 2: named event extraction engine. Knowl. Inf. Syst. **59**(2), 311–335 (2019)

13. Herman Tolentino, M., Raoul Kamadjeu, M., Michael Matters PhD, M., Marjorie Pollack, M., Larry Madoff, M.: Scanning the emerging infectious diseases horizon-visualizing promed emails using epispider. Adv. Dis. Surveill. **2**, 169 (2007)
14. Hersh, W.: Information Retrieval: A Health and Biomedical Perspective: A Health and Biomedical Perspective. Springer Science & Business Media (2008)
15. Joshi, A., Karimi, S., Sparks, R., Paris, C., MacIntyre, C.R.: Survey of text-based epidemic intelligence: A computational linguistic perspective. CoRR abs/1903.05801 (2019)
16. Kohlschütter, C., Fankhauser, P., Nejdl, W.: Boilerplate detection using shallow text features. In: Proceedings of the Third ACM International Conference on Web Search and Data Mining, pp. 441–450. ACM (2010)
17. Kumar, A., Patel, D., Jain, N.: Lightweight system for ne-tagged news headlines corpus creation. In: 2016 IEEE International Conference on Big Data, BigData 2016, Washington DC, USA, 5–8 December, 2016. pp. 3903–3912 (2016)
18. Lejeune, G., Brixtel, R., Doucet, A., Lucas, N.: Multilingual event extraction for epidemic detection. Artif. Intell. Med. **65**(2), 131–143 (2015)
19. Mazumder, S., Bishnoi, B., Patel, D.: News headlines: What they can tell us? In: Proceedings of the 6th IBM Collaborative Academia Research Exchange Conference (I-CARE) on I-CARE 2014, pp. 1–4. ACM (2014)
20. Mollema, L., et al.: Disease detection or public opinion reflection? content analysis of tweets, other social media, and online newspapers during the measles outbreak in the netherlands in 2013. J. Med. Internet Res. **17**(5), e128 (2015)
21. Sharma, S., Agrawal, A., Patel, D.: Class aware exemplar discovery from microarray gene expression data. In: Big Data Analytics - 4th International Conference, BDA 2015, Hyderabad, India, 15–18 December, 2015, Proceedings, pp. 244–257 (2015)
22. Singh, S.P., Khosla, S., Rustagi, S., Patel, M., Patel, D.: SL - FII: syntactic and lexical constraints with frequency based iterative improvement for disease mention recognition in news headlines, pp. 28–34 (2016)
23. Steinberger, R.: A survey of methods to ease the development of highly multilingual text mining applications. Lang. Resour. Eval. **46**(2), 155–176 (2012)
24. Steinberger, R., Pouliquen, B., der Goot, E.V.: An introduction to the Europe media monitor family of applications. CoRR abs/1309.5290 (2013)
25. Velasco, E., Agheneza, T., Denecke, K., Kirchner, G., Eckmanns, T.: Social media and internet-based data in global systems for public health surveillance: A systematic review. Milbank Q. **92**(1), 7–33 (2014)
26. Yan, S., Chughtai, A., Macintyre, C.: Utility and potential of rapid epidemic intelligence from internet-based sources. Int. J. Infect. Dis. **63**, 77–87 (2017)
27. Yangarber, R., Von Etter, P., Steinberger, R.: Content collection and analysis in the domain of epidemiology. In: Proceedings of DrMED-2008: International Workshop on Describing Medical Web Resources (2008)
28. Yom-Tov, E., Borsa, D., Cox, I.J., McKendry, R.A.: Detecting disease outbreaks in mass gatherings using internet data. J. Med. Internet Res. **16**(6), e154 (2014)
29. Yu, V.L., Madoff, L.C.: Promed-mail: An early warning system for emerging diseases. Clin. Infect. Dis. **39**(2), 227–232 (2004)

Author Index

Printed in the United States
By Bookmasters